Flagrant Fouls

Stephen Saine

RiverHouse
Publishing

Flagrant Fouls

RiverHouse Publishing, LLC
1509 Madison Avenue
Memphis, TN 38104

Copyright © 2015 by Stephen Saine

All rights reserved. No part of this book may be reproduced, stored in a retrieval system or transmitted in any form or by any means without written permission of the Publisher, excepting brief quotes used in reviews.

All **RiverHouse, LLC** Titles, Imprints and Distributed Lines are available at special quantity discounts for bulk purchases for sales promotions, premiums, fund-raising and educational or institutional use.

First RiverHouse, LLC Trade Paperback Printing 12-20-15

ISBN: 978-0-9962725-5-1

Report abuse to the FBI at www.fbi.gov.

www.riverhousepublishingllc.com

To my mother, Earnestine Lee
August 1, 1941-November 15, 2013

Acknowledgments

I would like to thank the Higher Heights Christian Church Family, Pastor James A. Adams, Pastor Leon Jones Jr., Pastor Terry L. Swain. I would also like to thank my family, friends and Danielle A. Jones

Foreword

"Death before Life"

Where does one draw the line? Who determines when enough is enough?

Stephen Saine portrays a hopeless lifestyle that was spiritually dead and headed for eternal destruction. At an early age, he was caught up in the fast lane—selling drugs to make quick and easy money. Many of his peers looked upon him as being very successful, but the price and penalty sustained in his line of business brought about life changing consequences.

He was bright and full of dreams but chose the wrong path to make those dreams a reality. He broke all the rules for selfish gain which was just a part of playing the game. In order to take on a new life, the author realized he had to die to his old habits and behavior. He had to do something different.

This book is an inspiring testimony of a young man that had several eye-opening encounters with his Creator and he knew without a shadow of a doubt that his life would end if he did not change his course of direction.

He is traveling a new highway now. His path of destruction has changed to a path that leads others to Christ. He works tirelessly telling men, women, boys, and girls that there is a better and more excellent way to success and happiness.

> -Linda M. Jamieson & Marilyn Ransom
> (Stephen's cousins)

When Stephen Saine was born, a Soldier entered the Atmosphere. One who came from the bottom of the world, to arise to a place where his light would shine. A Family Man pushed by the ills of Poverty to provide in a way that was not likened by Society. No excuses, but Facts of Survival. He Loved his Children and his Nephew. This book is not so much a snitch book, but it is an Information pamphlet. Trying to expose what really goes on with our Children and the sometimes Dark world of Sports. I can attest that Pastor Stephen Saine has experienced a Transformation from God and his WORD! One thing I'm impressed with is that he doesn't hide his Sins to expose others, he tells it like it is. Every Parent and Child that will experience the world of sports, needs a copy of this book in their possession. Great work!!!!

> -Pastor Leon Jones, Jr.

Table of Contents

Preface 10

Early Years 20

The Red Hunt 26

Pink Chevy 34

Caught 45

Never Going Back 55

Finally Answering the Call 59

Family 69

Pierre 83

Prelude to a Deal 95

Striking a Deal 104

Promises 117

Looking Back, Moving Forward 134

Preface

The Word of God as delivered through me:

Let them know I told you write these things that thou have done, seen and heard. Because these things are true and faithful it's in my word that you cannot but speak the things which thou have seen and heard.

Let them know that I still specialize in saving bad people like I tried to do the people of Sodom and Gomorrah, but they would not take heed and hearken to the warning, let them know that I am still not slack concerning my promise. Whatever I say I am able to bring it to pass I said ask and it shall be given, seek and you shall find, knock and the door shall be open. Let them know that it is not my will that any shall perish for wanting materialistic things.

So many people have allowed Satan to cloud their views and minds that they can have it other ways than through me, without having to suffer any repercussions. Tell them that they need to learn how to wait upon me; I am the one who gives all good and perfect gifts. Tell them I want to get to know them in an intimate way, and I want to have a never ending relationship with them and I want them to put whatever they are going through in my hands and leave it there. If you are going to pray why worry and if you are going to worry why pray?

Tell them they want me to do it all while they sit back and do nothing. According to the kingdom that is not good religion. They want me to save them and sanctify them, they want me to tell them to do it right and then they want me to make them do right. They want me to tell them to have faith and then they want me to give them the faith. They even want me to exercise the faith and cultivate the faith; leaving their efforts and actions at zero.

Still I want them to know: no faith no miracles; no burden no blessings; no work no pay; no cross no crown; no sadness no happiness; no confusion no peace; no weeping no smiling; no problem no solution; no questions no answers; no hurt no healing; no sickness no deliverance; no lost no found; no pressure no release; no emotion no control; no heart no feelings; no trouble no triumph; no weakness no strength; no failure no success; no darkness no light; no little no much; no frustration no security; no voice no comment; no fall no stand, no dying no living, no valleys no mountains, no alleys no avenues, no defeats no victory.

Tell them if they are not destroyed, let down, put down, set down, stepped on, and stepped over, talked about, lied on and lied to then they can't be remolded, reshaped, rejuvenated, or revealed. So learn to give God some of your time, whatever you need it is in the Bible. How in the world are you going to reach your goals, if you don't know your gift? Because your gifts are the things that help you reach your goals.

There are two ways to discover your gift. The first way is to see what people praise you for. If they praise you for singing, smiling, speaking, or creative art then maybe you have a gift for that. The other way to find your gift is to see what gets you in trouble. Anything that can get you in trouble means that you are gifted in that area. I know that I am right about this because I am speaking from personal experience.

I was sent to prison as a young man for persuading people to sell and buy drugs, but now I am persuading people to come to Christ. I am winning souls for the master by telling them the wages of sin is death but the gift of God is eternal life. So all I am saying to you now is that you can use what will get you in trouble and turn it into a blessing as I have.

Why would you use your gift negatively and suffer for it when you can use it positively and prosper from it? If you like to drive cars that do not belong to you, if you like to steal vehicles from others, why don't you become a parking attendant? If you like to strut and be seen and sell your body, why not become a model? If you like to fuss and argue, sow discord, why don't you become an orator or lawyer? If you like to cause physical harm to people, why not become a professional boxer? If you like messing with minds, why not become a psychiatrist?

So many people are busy trying to make a living until they are failing to make a life, and that life begins and ends with Jesus Christ. In other words, we try so hard to wear the best clothes, drive the finest cars, and live in the finest homes. We do that to only hear someone other than Jesus say these five little words, "You got it going on."

Some will work all the overtime there is on the job, but will not put in o.t. with God. I learned that is not sufficient enough for God. We are robbing him without a cause by not giving Him most of our time, when his is the one who allows us to have a job.

Take no thought for your life what ye shall eat or what ye shall drink, nor yet for your body, or what ye shall put on. I learned that you can have money in the bank, but your soul can be broke and bankrupt from no knowledge of Christ. You can have shoes on your feet and your soul can still be out of touch with Christ. You can have bread on your table but your soul can still be hungry for the word of God. Your stomach can be full but your soul can be malnourished.

I learned that there are some things money cannot buy. It can buy you a steak diner but it can't buy you an appetite. It can buy you a bed to sleep in but it can't buy you rest. It can't keep you from tossing and turning all night when you know you are living outside of His will.

I thought money would make me happy but what a fool I proved to be. I tell you the old proverb "a fool and his money are soon parted," is accurate. Whether it is in this life on Earth or the great Day of Judgment where your money can't do you any good. For what profit a man to gain the whole world and then lose his soul or what shall a man give in exchange for his soul?

I learned my soul is the most important thing I own. I learned if I lose my soul I have lost everything. Brothers and sisters I'm so glad I did not have to die first to see what my soul really meant to me. You remember the rich man that would not give Lazarus the crumb drops from his table in the book of Luke? Because he was rich and was looking out for himself not thinking about his neighbors all the while ignoring the commandment of God which instructs us to love your neighbor as yourself. Perhaps, he was not an avid Bible reader or perhaps he just did not care about the word of Jesus Christ.

He did not know the book of Matthew, 25: 32-46 because when I was hungry you fed me not, when I was in naked you clothed me not, when I was sick you visited me not, when I was in prison you came not unto me, to the least of my people you have done it to, you have also done it unto me. So he ended up in hell burning wanting another chance.

I tell you with tears in my eyes and hurt in my heart; listen to me, if you don't know Him in the pardons of your sins, give Him your life right now. When you are dead you can do no more. So I want to encourage your hearts to work while there is day because when night cometh no man can work. In other words love everybody and treat everybody the way you want to be treated. Keep the faith and stay on bending knees. In prayer give God all the praises; let a dying world know that for Christ, you die. Keep sowing good seeds so you can reap a good harvest so many people think that when you are dead you are dead but I want you to know that your grave is not the end of the story. The Bible said that it is appointed for man once to die and then face judgment. Yes you are going to be judged for the way you live on Earth and you are going to spend eternity in one of two places; eternal hell or eternal heaven.

I am able to truly say because I have surrendered all to Christ. I have been blessed more spiritually than monetarily. Money does nothing for the soul. I can lay down at night now without worrying about robbers kicking in my door, or police busting my house looking for drugs. What I have now, police cannot handcuff, robbers cannot steal or take, water cannot drown, and fire cannot burn. The world cannot take away me walking closer with Jesus. He walks with me, He talks with me, and He tells me I am his all. I don't have to worry any more about somebody setting me up for the kill because I learned when you are living that type of life all the odds are against you. You never know when you are going to breath your last breathe. You continue to think somebody is on your trail and your home going is just moments away.

In reality someone is actually on your trail. He goes by the name of Satan and he comes in all shapes and forms. In fact Satan has no more power over you than you allow him to have. We all know right from wrong and Satan is certainly not a representative of right. The love for money has kept you from trusting

God simply because you want everything now and Satan makes you think if it is not your way it's the wrong way because your way is the best way.

I want you to know whatever you are in, if you let go and let God have His way, He is able to bring you out and if you are out He is able to bring you in. The more I tried giving up the street life and selling drugs the deeper I became involved in Christ. It was like a three way tug-of-war, evil on one end, me in the middle, and good on the other end. The more I tried to pull away from evil and cling to good, the more evil would pull me back, and good would say "No, that is not the way. That way leads to death and destruction, eternal damnation. But if you do right, right will follow."

I allowed evil and wrong doing to be my guide. The repercussion of wrong is that I had to suffer in prison. Although I must admit I tried everything to get out of going to prison. The devil meant it for evil but God meant it for my good. It was in prison where my eyes opened for the first time without any major temptations. It was there were I learned that it could have been worse. There were some fellow inmates that had the same or a lesser charge than I had, still they were serving more time than me. It was in prison where God had begun to give me a sense of consideration. I learned that my dramatic life story is repeated daily in America and across the world. It has become an epidemic among young men yearning for the easy life by quitting school to be more like the person he sees on television.

Trapped in a poverty stricken environment, people began to admire the wealth and popularity of their neighborhood pimps, players, pushers, and thugs. They immediately began to take on this mind set and began to steal, kill, and destroy. They began to give into the odds that they feel are already against them and that is being African-American in America. They began to believe in what people close to them tell them they are nothing and will never amount to anything more than a thug.

I want to tell you that you are somebody and although you may be called nobody in the sight of men; in the eyes of God, you are somebody. So what if you came from a broken home or the projects? So what if you're grandparents raised you because your parents did not want you? You can still overcome despite your shortcomings. Jesus overcame living in the projects. Once a man asked, "How could any good come from Nazareth?" The more they talked the more Jesus fulfilled his purpose.

Remember the more people count you out the more God will count you in. Just stay humble and God will exalt you, but if you exalt yourself God will bring you down. I learned to quit listening to what people say because they will try to put your light out so theirs can shine instead. People used to tell me all the time I was nothing but a drug dealer and a whoremonger who would never change. Still God said I was right for a miracle and I want you to know that you are just right for a miracle. God is able to remake you and remold you. You are the clay and He is the potter. Just don't fight his will and let Him have His way and don't fight against His will. He will give you the ability to listen to and for His voice and not Satan's. When Satan speaks he lies but when God speaks His voice rings with nothing but truth.

Am I somebody because of who I know and what I own? Am I somebody because I am liked? If I'm not either of the previous am I unsuccessful or good for nothing? If I owned a lot of material things people will receive me for that Hand if I am penniless I am insignificant. The truth is I am somebody because God said I am somebody. When God made me in his image, at that moment I became so valuable to him that he made a way that whatever I want I can ask in Jesus' name and if it's his will it shall be given to me.

I know what is best for me and nothing or no one can change that because God so loves me that He gave His only begotten son to die for me and my hang-ups. He knows and has forgotten my past so I will let him guide my future. I thought I knew what was best for me by letting the streets and Satan guide my life which landed me in prison. But I was grateful for it because I had time to sit and think about how God held His harsh justice back and gave me mercy and another chance at life. Before giving myself to God, like the rich young ruler mentioned in Luke 12:16-21, I thought I had done well for myself because of all the money I accumulated without working honestly for it.

For many years I had put up a certain amount of money, and with the rest of it, I ate, shopped, and

Flagrant Fouls

migrated where I wanted and when I wanted, while buying who I wanted and when I wanted. I can now look back on it and tell God thank you for not cutting me down and saying these words unto me, "thou fool this night thou soul shall be required of thee then who shall those things be which Satan has provided for you when I was trying to tell you to submit yourself to me and resist the devil and he will flee. You would not listen." So I am thankful he didn't take that action on me. I thank him for being a first chance God, a second chance God, a third chance God, a fourth chance god, and last but not least another chance God.

Early Years

Memphis, Tennessee, my place of birth, has changed a great deal since I was born in 1970 to now 2010. The city has its share of critics. For example, in February 2010 Forbes ranked it as the third most miserable city in the United States. I'm certainly not saying the city is perfect, but Memphis has many revealing qualities.

Boys and girls from all over the world come to the city to receive treatment for cancer at the St. Jude Children's Research Hospital in Memphis. And every time I hear a report about how the cure rate has improved over the years; it makes me proud to call the place that houses that amazing facility, founded by the late Danny Thomas, home.

FedEx, the world's leading overnight shipping service is located in Memphis. The city has so many organizations like, MIFA, Legal Service Center, Senior Service Center, established to serve those in need, that its sometimes mind boggling.

You don't have to look far to find a church either, there's more in Memphis than any other city in Tennessee. There's a reason it's referred to as the Bible Belt. There's a diverse population of people in the Big M also including African-Americans, Hispanic- Americans, Asian-Americans, and White-Americans. There are people of the Jewish Faith,

Hindus, Buddhists, Protestants, Muslims, just name the group and they are represented in Memphis. It also has great support for its college basketball team, but I'll get to that later. You would never know about the highs of the city speaking to some of its very own residents though. Some people will only offer you doom and gloom. With some of the residents there's an inferiority complex. I'm sure some of this comes from transplants while the rest is spin from city natives who want to get out of it.

Funny, several people in many of the nearby small towns look at Memphis as a place of opportunity while others in those same areas wouldn't go twenty miles near it. I've realize people are all different and all the same regardless where you go. It's not where you are from; it's how you treat people.

My mother, Earnestine McNeil-Lee is from Somerville, one of those small towns not far from Memphis I was referring to. When she had my twin sister, Stephanie and I, she was living in Memphis. My mom was always the rock of the family until she passed away in 2013. Those of us in the African-American community are all too familiar with this. During the later quarter of the past century to present, women have played the role of the matriarch and the patriarch in Black families. My mom was no different.

Shortly after we were born she moved us to Somerville. We moved back to Memphis when my sister and I were about five years of age. My mom had six of us in all. Early in life I had a strong relationship with my oldest brother and sister, Eddie Niles and Rubystine Niles. My bond with Rubystine would change drastically over the years.

My father, Jimmy Saine, lived in Fayette County near Memphis. He and my mother never married. In fact, he had a family of his own there. While in Somerville I attended Central Elementary during my kindergarten year and first grade. My grandmother and uncles were living in Memphis in a neighborhood known as Binghampton so we had a support network in place when my mom decided to move back to Memphis. Once back, I enrolled at Bruce Elementary for two years. Then my mom was married and moved us from an apartment in Mid-Town Memphis to a house north of the city in a section called Raleigh.

Every Sunday I attended church with my mom. Regardless of what was going on in my life, I made sure I was giving praises to the Lord on the Sabbath. Even as kid, people suspected I would someday play a larger role in the church. One day a friend and I were asked to give a short speech about Easter. When the time came for us to talk, he ran out faster than Usain Bolt. Gone faster than you could say, "Come back." I delivered my speech without a hitch, leaving some in attendance convinced that it would be the start of something greater.

School wise, I started attending this nearby elementary named Scenic Hill and remained there through my sixth grade year. I was a good grade school student. I read anything put in my face. I enjoyed knowledge. I was good at math. Unfortunately, I enjoyed attention just as much. I wanted to be the class clown and I wanted to standout. I moved on to Treadwell Middle School/Junior High. Things changed dramatically. My focus shifted. I didn't participate in many school extracurricular activities like sports. Instead I was getting into trouble and fighting.

I attended Treadwell high school and sat in the same class room with perhaps the best basketball player to ever come out of Memphis, Anfernee "Penny" Hardaway. One day there was this White kid getting under Penny's skin, calling him "nigger," and then had the nerve to lick his fist and strike him. Penny was on the basketball team and was trying to stay out of trouble. This, of course, was before the age of the internet and instant information. Still, somehow it seemed like whatever Penny did made the news. Although he was admired by just about everybody at school, no one wanted their life to be under a constant microscope at the age of 15 and 16.

I could tell he wanted to retaliate after being hit so I edged him on. I told Penny, "hit him back!" He was so shy then, yet smart enough to realize he was in a no win situation. I wasn't though. The way I saw it, at least at the time, I had nothing to lose. I assured Penny, "I'm gonna hit him back. He called you a nigger and he hit you." Later that day a friend of mine and I beat the kid senseless with sticks. Word of this fight made its way to the school principal. He asked Penny what happened. He didn't want to rat me out but he had to tell the truth. The principal asked Penny if I'd hit the kid. Penny hung his head low then gave an honest account of the events.

My friend/accomplice received a home suspension, essentially meaning he was sent home from school, but could return back in a few days. I, however, was given a board suspension because it was probably my third fight of the year. I was out of school for a much longer period and had to go to the Board of Education to appeal my case so I could be reinstated into school. Deservingly so, Penny avoided any trouble for his role in the incident. He and I still look back and laugh about it to this day.

Unlike Penny, I stayed in trouble at that school. I once tried to set another student on fire. This kid, named Jimmy Malone, for some reason decided he wanted to sit in my desk and when I asked him to get up he would not comply. Jimmy was a big bully. I hit him hard enough to break his glasses but he remained steadfast to his position and refused to get up. I hit him again and his pale colored skin was suddenly replaced with a shade of red. Still he did not budge. I'm thinking to myself, "Oh, you are going to get up." So I took out my cigarette lighter, lit the paper on his desk which of course began to spread, and wala, like magic he was up. That stunt led to a board suspension. The only reason I was able to get back in school was because my mom was a great parent who had established a great relationship with the schools' administrators. I know they had to be wondering how in the world a sweet woman, like my mother produce such a vile high school student like me.

The environment in high school was so different than in grade school. We were not with one teacher all day like in elementary and we had so much more freedom. Some of the instructors talked to us like we were adults. If grades were tangible, they would have been slipping right out of my hands. As it was, things were certainly slipping out of my control and all the while I continued to be a distraction at school. And to think, problems at school were the least of my issues.

The Red Hunt

Now all these things happened unto them for examples: and they are written for our admonition, upon whom the ends of the world are come. Wherefore let him that thinketh he standeth take heed lest he fall. 1 Corinthians 10:11 – 12

In this life, snares and traps are set as a demonic plan and trap. This is a warning against some of the ills that are out there to hinder a person. This is not a life that one should parallel; however, the capability of a person being entrapped is there. No one is exempt so don't say... this can't happen to me. Please don't put too much confident in yourself because many people are powerless against some vises. It is important to develop a relationship with God.

Tipton is a county located just North of Memphis. The county seat is Covington, which is also one of its largest towns, although there are only about 10,000 residents. Even smaller is a town in Tipton named Mason which, according to the 2000 U.S. Census report, had less than 2,000 people. But never judge a book by its cover or in this case a town by the number of people residing therein. On the weekend that numbered ballooned as people from nearby counties and the state of Arkansas and Mississippi traveled to the small town of Mason to party, to get wild, to just have fun. Word spread about a strip of clubs located in Mason which included the Green Apple, the Real Deal, Club Taymay, Club House Party, and the club my mother owned called The Red Hut.

My mom honed her club managing skills in Somerville after being part owner of one with my father. She eventually decided to break out and manage one of her own. Why not, she had amazing business sense and with her girl next door personality, she was quite the host. She knew how to make people feel at home. Customers, some even older than my mother, called her mom. The Red Hut appealed to people of many races. Most of the customers were Black, but it had its fair share of Hispanics, and Whites also. It was a nice size building with concrete floors and a huge lounge in the front for mingling and dancing. There was a smaller room in the back where people would retreat to for small time gambling with dice and the like.

The music was a mix of R&B, blues and some contemporary stuff as well. It wasn't unusual for bands to perform live or for a DJ to be present. Local rapper Skinny Pimp entertained the crowd one night. That club was always packed. Saturdays and Sundays were HUGE nights. There were times it would get so packed my mom would have to shut it down to keep from violating fire codes. My mom learned early on how things could get out of hand when there were large numbers of people mixed with alcohol, but more important, she knew how to take control of situations and calm things down. There were times she had to go to the extreme to keep the peace. Not only have I seen my mom pull a gun. I've seen her shoot it. A guy name Ricky was one of the many people who referred to her as "mom" and was at the club one calm night when some guys from Galloway were looking for trouble. They began jumping on Ricky in the middle of the club. My mom came from the back of the gambling hole, "What's going on?"

"We're gonna whip this nigga!" they replied, claiming he wronged one of them. "It doesn't take all of you to jump on him," she said. "You can get out of here with that nonsense." Talking to them apparently didn't help because they continued their pursuit of him. All of a sudden the chaos turned into complete silence after my mom pointed her gun. Pow! Pow! Pow! Yet the silence was only temporary. One of the Galloway three wanted to test my mom.

"Rush her," he said. "Those are just blanks," or so he thought.

She pointed at him and said, "You'll be the first to go if you think they're blanks." She turned the gun away from him and toward the wall and fired another shot. The large hole left and the smoking cloud hovering it spoke clearer than anything my mom would have been able to say to them. They got the point.

Since I was the youngest male child and there was such a big gap in age between my brother and me, my mother thought it would be best if she kept an eye on me so she often took me with her to the Red Hut on the weekends. What she didn't know is that I was taking it all in, consuming and learning about the tricks and the trades of the business. I had fully embraced the night life, or as Donna Summers once put it in song, the "Street Life."

One night while going to buy ice cream, I walked by one of the clubs just down the street from my mom's place. I just happened by a bag on the ground, it was a money bag full of the good old green. I estimate it was probably worth $80,000 in cash and food stamps. I grabbed it, thinking about all the things I could do with it, and took it straight to my mom's club and gave it to her. She knew right off who it belonged to. The owner of the money had been looking for the bag that night and my mom knew her, so she took it straight to her. Finding that kind of money is like a test from above. It really makes you ponder about things. Believe me all sorts of things were going through my mind. Add that to seeing guys riding around the neighborhood in their big cars, fancy clothes, jewelry, and shooting dice with stacks of cash, it all became too enticing for me to pass up. I wanted my share of that.

Some days my mom would make the trek to Mason without me. No problem, I was able to get my night life fix in a small little community in North Memphis, called James Sub. There were several drug dealers in that neighborhood and of course when you have idle time on your hands like I did it was easy to pick up on what they were doing. I was in the 10th grade attending Treadwell High at the time when I met this big drug dealer nicknamed Tah Tah. He was heavy. He was the man. Everybody would go to Tah Tah to get drugs. I use to hang out with his nephew. One day his nephew had this powder like substance on him. I asked him what it was and he gave me the low down. We went to his aunt's house, who was also Tah Tah's sister, and she gave us a 101 lesson on powder cocaine. She showed us how to cook it up, and distribute it. She told us how much to sell it for, how much to keep, and most important, as far as she was concerned, what percent of money to bring back to her. We learned and we acted on what we learned. It came easy to us, if only learning in the classroom were as simple. Tah Tah's sister owned both a Bronco and a drop-top Mustang. We had access to the Mustang and would drive to high school football and basketball games, although neither of us had a license. As you can imagine we felt like the real "Hot Boys." We began hanging out around the local dope track selling crack cocaine to any and everybody who wanted it.

I remember working the track one day in the rain and some guy came through in a van. He said, "Hey man give me a twenty; give me a fat one now." For those street challenged, twenty refers to the going rate for a particular amount of the product being sold. So I leaned into the vehicle to give him the product and he took off driving. The way I looked at it, that was my money invested in that dope so I held on to the van as he continued to drive. I started beating on the van and he started to drive faster so eventually I had to jump off to avoid getting seriously injured. I was livid. Apparently he wasn't too smart. There were not many White people in James Sub to begin with, yet he decides to show his face again two days later as if I wouldn't spot him. Maybe he thought because he was in a different vehicle I wouldn't recognize him. Wrong. My friend and I started throwing bricks at his ride, busting his windows and damaging his exterior. We never saw that guy again.

Now I was failing at school but more than holding my own in the drug game. If that sounds familiar, it's because it has become a common story for some inner city kids in Memphis. The graduation rate for Memphis City School students dropped from an already disappointing 66.9 to a paltry 62.1 percent. Under Federal mandate, the goal for Memphis was 74.6. Memphis is one of many cities in the

United States struggling with graduating students. New York City celebrated graduating 59 percent of students there in 2009 and that was an increase from 56 percent the year before. Now what do you think happens to all of those kids who do not graduate. All of them do not stray down the wrong path, but I can guarantee you the majority of them do. I had graduated from dealing in rocks and started buying ounces which at the time cost me about $800 per ounce but as you can imagine I was able to flip it into much more. Unbeknownst to my mother I started taking my product with me when I went with her to the club in Mason. I was selling crack in that small country town. Now my mom knew I had money, but she assumed I was getting it from an honest day's work. My cover was yard service. Heck, I saved enough money from cutting grass to buy my first moped, so I reasoned it would at the minimum, by me sometime until the truth was uncovered. Meanwhile, I was doing good business in Mason, but of course wanted to expand. That's the thing about being successful, in whatever you do, legit or not, the more you experience it the more you want, so expansion was only logical in my eyes. My cousin, a couple friends of mine and I would break away from Mason, especially when it was slow and drive about 15 minutes to Covington and set up shop there as well. Some nights we would leave Covington and drive to Rossville, the home of the late Blues and bottle neck guitar great Fred McDowell. When either of those places were slow we traveled to Ripley. We would be listening to the song that had become my unofficial anthem, "I've Got a Pocket Full of Stones." How apropos as I was on my way to sell "stones" or rocks of my own. My name started growing and before I knew I was "the man."

Pink Chevy

For whosoever will save his life shall lose it; but whosoever shall lose his life for my sake and the gospel's, the same shall save it. Mark 8:35

There are always consequences when you are drawn away by your own lust and don't observe to the trouble and danger signs. The streets have a way to draw you in, fast money keeps you in, and reputation gives you a false sense of security. The Bible tells us that if we hold fast to these things your life will ultimate be lost. However, developing a relationship with God, repenting of your sins, and follow the writings in the gospel shall save his life. You want to take advantage of the plan God has for you. Its reward has benefits now and in eternity.

Flagrant Fouls

I was making so much money by the time I reached the 11th grade some of my teachers were asking me to borrow money. Although I never sold drugs at school, I assume people knew because my lifestyle and cash flow began to change. My 11th grade year would be my last in high school. Because I failed the 11th grade I decided to call it quits and dropped out of high school.

As the years passed, I was really doing it. I became quite the salesman. The key is that I was very loyal to my customers so in return they became very loyal to me. There were times my customers wouldn't have the money so I would front it to them. I offered more credit than I received payments up front. Still they would always pay me. They respected me because I wasn't some dope boy talking crazy to them and acted as if I was better than them because they were users. It really made a difference because when I couldn't make it out of Memphis, they would come to me even if they were miles away in Millington, Covington, and Ripley. They would ask, "Where Steve at?" They would also ask for me by my street name, "Where's Pink Chevy?" The pink Chevy was even logging miles in Holly Springs, Mississippi and West Memphis, Arkansas. Branching out really made me successful at what I was doing. I couldn't do it all, so I started recruiting people, including family members to help me move the product. I was having some of it shipped through the mail via UPS. Sometimes all I had to do is wake up in the morning go to the door and receive my shipment. I would be up all night counting my money.

When my oldest brother lived on the West Coast, he developed a friendship with a guy who sold drugs. I purchased from this guy once when he decided to come along with my brother and pay a visit to Memphis. I bought about $10,000 worth of dope from him. He liked the fact that he could get that kind of money instantly. He then suggested that when he travels back to California we continue to do business. He asked if I would be willing to give him the money up front and he would mail me the stuff when he reached Cali. I don't think so. I told him, "I ain't giving you no money to go back up the road and I don't really know you like that. Even if I did know you, I'm not sending money like that. Now if you want to trust me with the goods and then I send you the money, we can roll like that." He went back home and called me two days later telling me to be on the lookout for the UPS truck. A few mornings later he asked me if I had gone outside to check the mail. "Yeah," I told him, "there's nothing there." He paused, "Well there will be, so stay on the lookout." Twenty minutes later, a UPS driver pulled up in front of the house. The UPS worker dropped off a very big box. When I opened it, I saw nothing but clothes and shoes for toddlers. There was also two smaller boxes of washing powder. "This ain't the Goodwill Industries," I thought to myself. I called him to get an explanation. He told me to open the washing powder boxes and dig down deep in it. I opened both boxes and found a key of cocaine in each. My connection in California ended after a short stint, however when he got caught.

Still, along with my Jeri Curl, my pink Chevy was my calling card. It was actually an old rust colored Chevy when I purchased it. Essentially I just bought a body and then put some wheels on it, had it primed, got it painted, added new seats, put in a radio, and put a blue top on it. Before pink Chevy I owned a canary colored one. It was expensive to make so many modifications to the pink Chevy but I was making so much money that it didn't matter. Blasting out of the speakers of the pink Chevy were songs from local rappers like Pretty Tony and Gangsta Pat, founders of the dance M.C. Hammer would later introduce to the world as the "get buck," what people in Memphis had long known as the "gangsta walk." Of course their music represented my life style because I thought I was a gangster, and just like the gangsters glamorized in various circles of the hip-hop, culture I had my share of run ins with the police.

The most explosive scene was during a calm night in Covington. Calm until my posse and I arrived. So much happened that night as egos went unchecked, tempers exploded; too much testosterone no doubt. It ended with the police shooting at us and us shooting at the police. If it was a boxing match there would have been hugging all night without a referee to separate use, because fortunately no one was shot.

Representatives from the narcotics department came out on the Millington track one day. Several of us were standing there in big snow suits, which at the time were in style, when the Narcs rolled up. One of the undercover officers popped out and said he was looking for Pink Chevy. "I'm cool," he said. "Y'all can sell me something," he added. "Pink Chevy sells me stuff all the time." One of my boys looked over at me as if to ask, "Do you know this fool?" I just shook my head. Obviously we didn't do any business with him and we took off running.

A week later they came back to Millington with a warrant and bust into a house I use to stand in front of selling. But I didn't have any dealings with that particular house. I was usually at the house next door so they were looking for me at the wrong house. Regardless, on the day they came looking for me in Millington, I was in Mason and the word got back to me and I was told it would be smart if I didn't come near Millington. "They said they were looking for Pink Chevy," someone told me. So I stayed away for at least a week. Better luck next time.

Hearing they were after me didn't put any fear in me. I was young and cocky with no fear. I really didn't rationalize what I was doing. I didn't look at what life was and I didn't value my life. It was all about the money, the quick dollar and my growing popularity. My clientele consisted of doctors, lawyers, police officers, Hispanics, Whites, Blacks, city

Flagrant Fouls

employees, women who wanted to do tricks, and even politicians.

So many customers, so much drugs, and yet no one could catch me. I was always one step ahead of the police. As far as I'm concerned, I invented the key magnet for drug smuggling. People who are still dealing in drugs in Memphis will say, "Steve came out with that." The key magnet of course was invented for people to keep up with their keys. I put rocks in it and hid it up under my car. You could have 50 to 60 rocks at a time ride wherever and they wouldn't fall. The police would stop me and search me and inside my car but the rocks were under the vehicle. They are probably hip to that now. A friend of mine would say years later, "Steve you use to come up with all kinds of tricks on the tracks. Do you remember when you came out with the key magnet?" Everybody started doing the key magnet with the rocks in it after that.

When I advance to heavier stuff or "weights" and stop messing with rocks, I would buy three or four key magnets. If I was going to Covington or Mason to deliver the goods I would take ounces at a time and put them in sandwich bags. It would fit in a little key magnet, so what I would do is take the sandwich bag and tie it up and stick it in the key magnet and force it a bit, and what couldn't fit would just hang out of the magnet. I would take that and stick it to my back Chevy bumper and it wouldn't move. If the key magnet had moved the dope would move and vice-versa, but the key magnet was that good and it never went anywhere, it was just that solid. I was able to haul ounces at a time under my bumper. The police and I would get into full-fledged conversations about the pink Chevy when they pulled me over because they couldn't find what they were really looking for. They would always tell me, "I like your car." I would just smile and laugh inside while thinking, "I know what you're looking for. But I'm not about to tell you where it's at. You'll just have to work for it to find it."

I really made the police's job hard too. One day in Mason, while at my mother's club, a guy I use to gamble with lost all of his money shooting craps and began to act out, throwing and breaking chairs. I was about 27 years of age at the time and a bit more mature so I asked the guy nicely to not throw any more of my mother's chairs. He replied, "Fuck you Steve. Ain't nobody scared of you no more. You're always shooting at these other guys. Shoot your pistol at me." I told him I didn't have any beef with him, and was just letting him know the chairs were too expensive for him to be tossing them away like junk mail. "This ain't your club," he shot back, "this yo' momma club." He didn't realize that I had purchased the chairs, and as far as I was concerned, it didn't matter who bought them, it was my mom's club. "Just don't throw another down." He just kept running his mouth and the Memphis thug was begging to come out of me. I didn't want to whip him up in front of my mom, who had a cooler head than I at the time and ask me to just walk away. All

the while I'm thinking "if he says one more thing...."
Of course he did and that's when the fight began.

I beat him like a drum stick. Eddie Murphy once joked when you get beat up you have to one up the person who did the deed. "You're dead man," Murphy said mimicking the guy on the wrong end of the fight. Apparently there's truth in fiction because this guy threatened to do the same. "I'm finnah go get my gun," he yelled. He stayed in the Mason area so he didn't have far to go to try to make good on his promise. That's when my mom, who owned a gun herself, stepped in. She told him, "you go get a gun for my boy I'm going to have to kill you."

"That's alright mom," I said. "I'm going to get my gun." I jumped in my Cadillac on my way to Memphis to get my piece. It was already a bad day for me because someone saw me hiding some ounces behind my mom's club and when I came back to get it, nothing, because it was stolen. I had blown a sale. My strategy was to always leave something in the Mason area just in case someone from nearby like Ripley beeped me hoping to make a transaction. I would meet the person at an undisclosed location or either at my mother's club. So I was already boiling about that and here's this guy in my mom's club acting a fool and talking about taking me out.

I got to Highway 70 just before making it to Gallaway, Tennessee when I got a call from my oldest sister. She didn't mince words with me either. She said, "Look, you need to get home right now. Narcotics are all in the house. They're in your bedroom, they've got your gun on the table." And to think, I was on my way to the house to get the gun. She continued, "They've got your money on the table. They've got your chains out and they've got your weed." I asked her, "Do they have something else?" I was trying to be discreet because I didn't want to say anything on the phone in case the phone was bugged. I thought maybe they had found the big stuff, the keys of coke I was getting in through the mail from California. I knew it would take a minute to find that if they did.

Good thing they didn't bring any sniffing hounds because I made a hole in my closet wall were I had perfectly cut out a board I could just pull out and put back. The average eye couldn't pick it up, nor could the Narcs. But I knew that's what they were looking for. There were six keys in there, nestled down in the wall with about $200,000 in cash. I would be in jail to this day if they had found it. Was I concerned when I walked into the house? Yes, but I was cool as a cucumber. As soon as I stepped through the door the investigators were asking if I was Steve Saine. They told me I was going to jail and they had been on my tail for some time.

All the while I'm looking at what they have laid out on the table including six thousand dollars. Earlier that day one of my customers from Covington whom I had given credit, came by to pay me. I was about to leave the house that day with it in my pocket to gamble with but my mom suggested I should leave it behind and there was no need for me

Flagrant Fouls

to take all that money on me. So I took a small portion of the money with me and left six grand between my bed matrices. They found it and as my sister warned, they had the marijuana sitting out. They also had my gun. No cocaine.

The weed they found was about 3-tenths of an ounce worth. The scene was surreal because there were cameras with the police. They were filming an episode of the popular television show *COPS*. I was very familiar with the theme song, "Bad boys bad boys...whatcha gonna do, whatcha gonna do when they come for you," but I'd never thought I would make a cameo appearance.

The officers at my house that night were bold and cocky. They were trying to pressure me to admitting I sold cocaine. I'm not sure if the cameras were still filming during that time. Regardless I wasn't about to incriminate myself. So they asked me to explain where all the money came from.

"I've been gambling," I told them. I was lying of course, but hey what did they have on me besides some chronic. As a result, they questioned me about distributing weed. "Every now and then I sell," I told them, "I smoke it too." This was strategic of course because I wasn't a pot-smoker. But by admitting to something it would help throw them off. At worse, they probably figured I was selling weed all the time yet they had no solid evidence. This changed their focus from the powdered stuff to the grassy stuff. The powdered stuff gets you more time behind bars.

A bit disappointed, one of the cops said they would write me a citation for the gun and take the money and weed back to the station. They also told me I'd have to appear in court. I begin pressing my luck because I didn't want to give up six-thousand. "Why are ya'll taking my money?" I asked. "That little weed you found, that's personal use," I continued. One of the officers was in agreement with me and said they should give me my money back, but the other apparently wanted to inconvenience me just as I had inconvenienced them. So they took it or should I say stole it. I got the citation and made arrangements to go to court to get my money back. When I get to court, what's on the books is far less than the six-thousand they left my house with. They had only turned in one-thousand five hundred. It probably wasn't even worth all of the effort to get the $1,500 because I paid my lawyer nine-hundred to get it. I guess I should not have been too upset seeing that I figuratively dodged a bullet. Once again I proved too elusive for the men and women in the blue uniforms. As always I was one step ahead of them, or so I thought.

Caught

Grace be with you all. Amen. Hebrew 13:25

I know you've heard do the crime and you do the time; however, God's grace will step in and do what no other can do. His grace is unmerited favor. Although I didn't deserve it, God looked beyond my faults and He saw my need. Ultimately, God knows what we shall be now what we appear to be. His grace is sufficient.

All the best laid plans I had of avoiding being caught meant absolutely nothing. The Bible reads "you reap what you sow." Just like everyone else running afoul of the law, my time was coming too.

I was becoming so heavy that it was only a matter of time before the police came looking for me. The only real way to keep a secret is to not tell anyone, not a soul. Obviously that can never be the case if you are selling drugs. Your supplier knows, your customers know. And if either one of those components of the drug paradigm were to crumble, chances are the person who is at the very center of it all, in this case the seller, becomes vulnerable as well.

In most of the gangster mob movies the very thing that brings down a so called drug empire is either jealousy or trust and sometimes those two run in accord. Trust is such an important part of the entire operation on every level of the game. Sometimes trust is established through word of mouth; with a person you already trust telling you that the next person is good on their word. Sometimes trust is built over time and you gain confidence in the person you are around. Trust is also instinctual at times. Some people you just have a good vibe about while others you do not. Still, none are 100 percent full proof methods of determining who you can trust, especially out in the streets. I received an advanced lesson in this the hard way.

I received my first of three charges back in 1992. A guy called me and requested three ounces of the product. I had already sold everything I had on me so I had to go re-up or re-stock. So I called a friend of mine and asked him to bring me the three ounces. He delivered and I asked my step father, who was working with the Shelby County Sheriff's Office, to take me to make the sell. My friend was trying to be greedy and meet the person making the purchase so he could bargain with him in the future. I was on to his plan. So my stepdad drove me, my friend and the guy who turned out to be the informant to a MAPCO Express in North Memphis to hook up with the buyer. When we get there the buyer is nowhere in sight. "Where is he," I ask. So the insider gets on the pay phone and calls him. Still no show.

I'm beginning to feel a bit apprehensive. "Something's going on, let's roll," I tell my step dad. But the informant jumps in the car with an update. "They said to meet them at the McDonald's farther down the road." Ignoring intuition we drove there and waited. The informant gets out of the car and gets on a phone again. He became very animated and started waving, "here they come." We thought he was signaling them over instead he was using code letting them know we had drugs in the vehicle. Less than 30 seconds later I had a gun pointed at me. The police lights were so bright it was hard to make out any of them, but I could tell they were everywhere. "Get out the car," I heard one of them shout. "You too," another hollered at my stepdad. Since he worked for the Sherriff's office he showed them his badge, but that only made matters worse. "You're in it to!" another one declared. As far as they were concerned he was an accessory to the crime. For my stepfather's sake, what they didn't know is that he was a quasi-customer of mine. He smoked primos and whenever he made runs for me I would pay him in cash or in drugs. He was the only person in the department I served. There were also a host of local politicians calling me to satisfy their drug craze. Needless to say, my stepfather lost his job. We were taken down to the jailhouse but were released on bond the next morning.

You would think going to jail would have deterred me from further dealings of the underworld. Nope. Not me. I reasoned it was my first charge and I knew I would get nothing more than probation. I was correct, I received three years and I was relieved. However had they caught me with three ounces of hard rock cocaine instead of powder I would have certainly received time and sent to federal prison. Plus the dope was not mine. They saw my friend toss the drugs in the backseat when they bum rushed us and could not prove I was the owner.

Now I did become a bit more selective and discreet with whom I sold to after being placed on probation. But I would eventually let my guard down.

When I was busted the second time it was again because someone I thought I could trust, a family friend, set me up. In Mason, a guy who spent a great deal of time at my mother's club and a great deal of time buying crack from me was working with undercover cops. They had evidence on him already but were willing to look away if he could help them catch the big fish, me. He would request and I would supply him with large quantities that he would deliver to the undercover agents. He was taking thorough notes of each transaction. Each time he purchased from me he would go write my name down with the date and time of the exchange. That turned out to be one indictment.

I'll admit, I became cocky which of course leads to a feeling of invincibility and that leads to carelessness. One of the undercover policemen actually approached me himself and then introduced me to his law enforcement partner, who was also working undercover. By doing this they eliminated the family friend, or the middle man, and began dealing with me directly. I sold them huge amounts of cocaine. There was an occasion where they were request an amount larger than usual. I was in Memphis at the time one of the undercover agents called me and asked me to come out to Mason. I told him he would have to come to Memphis. He said he couldn't and I told him we would just have to postpone the deal until another day.

The following weekend I went out to the Red Hut. Late into the night we closed the club down as usual. I got into my Cadillac headed back to Memphis when a host of police officers flagged me down and pulled me over. They asked me to step out of the car. "What's going on?" I asked. That's when they hit me with the news, I was being arrested for selling drugs. They apprehended me and took me to jail. I ended being tried in criminal court. I made another effort to one-up the system by paying an informant, who was on the take, not to come to court. I paid him about $8,000. It was not money well spent. The prosecutors applied the pressure, telling him if he didn't show up in court they were going to arrest him on the evidence they had accumulated on him. He showed up to court and pointed me out to the jury. I didn't even get a refund from him. The undercover cop identified me as well. I was sentenced to prison for eight years. I know that's not a life sentence, but as far as I was concern it may as well had been.

Again I tried my luck with the system and applied for a time cut or a reduction in my sentence for the time I had been in the slammer awaiting a transfer. Instead I was hit with papers informing me I had "add-ons," meaning new charges. Are you serious? I didn't know where this was coming from, but they were quick to educate me on them. This secret indictment was courtesy of the City of Memphis. It came about because of another friend of the family, a guy one of my sisters dated in high school. This guy would come by the house every morning like a newspaper delivery person and buy dope from me. Now I knew this guy was supposed to be doing weekend time so I questioned him about it. He told me he was being allowed to leave early because of the good behavior. I was thirsting for money so bad I was dehydrated so I didn't think much of his answer actually. But my dope was going from my hand to his hand to the hands of the police, giving me my third charge.

I just knew I was going to be locked up forever. With my new charge my number of years leaped to a total of 12. Then I heard about prison boot camp patterned after the military designed to modify problem behavior. Completing the course also meant a decrease in time. I had to fire my first attorney who did not believe it would be possible for me to be accepted into the boot camp based on the number of charges I had. My new lawyer promised me he would get me into boot camp, but talk is cheap. The clock continued to tick, time continued to move, and I continued to rot in my cell. I decided to call upon the only someone I knew had the power and authority to get me into boot camp. I got on my knees and I prayed to God. I told Him, "When I get out of here, I'm through God. I'm not messing with no more drugs, I'm through. I promise you if you can just deliver me from here. I'm going preach your word. I'm going to do what you called me to do. I know I've been running from you but I'm going to do it."

Then one morning out of the blue I heard a guard say, "Saine, pack your bags!" I knew what that mean. I was about to roll out of there. I was headed to boot camp. Four months and I'm headed home. God is good. The other inmates were telling me how I would hate boot camp. They said I would have to shave my head and they'll talk to you anyway they please. "Those white folks in Clifton, Tennessee, they are dirty," one said about the site of the boot camp.

Inmates noted that several people came from boot camp right back to the penitentiary. I knew they were not exaggerating. I had seen enough guys leave only to come back a few weeks later, proof of their testimony. But I was going to be different I told them. Because four months is better than twelve years.

When I arrived at the boot camp site and stepped off the bus, I was greeted with officers calling me son-of-a-this and mother-that. They were all in my face screaming, spitting. I knew I had to remain mentally strong to survive it. Being blatantly treated like a second class citizen was a lot for a 24-year-old to swallow. I had to run miles every day and climb 40 foot ropes for the heck of it.

The funny thing about life is that there is division everywhere you go, even in prison. There were guys locked up who were from the East side of Tennessee and they did not like the guys from the West side of the state and vice-versa. Stupid mess.

This cadet from the Knoxville area they called Juvenile had it in for me. He would report me to the higher ups for any and everything I did. I knew if I fought him while in boot camp I would be sent straight back to the pen, so like an elementary kid telling another kid, "I'm going to get you after school," I told Juvenile he was mine when I got out of camp. But the animosity ended when it was time to graduate and move on. We were so happy to have made it through that we didn't even consider fisti-cuffs or anything like that. Twelve years probation, here I come. And as it turns out, I enjoyed the experience. I was in no rush to get home as I had become one of their favorite cadets and rose to the ranks of a platoon leader.

After I got out of boot camp, I probably did right for about three months, but being broke and disgusted at opportunities for a convicted felon, I revisited my old ways. I had been dealing drugs since high school so it was all I knew. I got my G.E.D. at boot camp but I just did not have an area of expertise or work experience for that matter. I did tone it down a bit because I did not want to get caught with cocaine so I started dealing in pounds of marijuana. I knew if caught the charges would be far less severe. You would be surprised how much people who have been through the jail system learn about the legal system.

Through my girlfriend's brother I was introduced to this youngster from Dallas he knew name Julio. He was in Memphis selling weed. I was broke so I asked him for an advance on some but he wouldn't give it to me. When I can look back on this now I can say this was a smart move, but then I was filled to the rim with selfishness and decided to just rob him for his weed. He pulled his gun out and I reached for mine. We began running and shooting at one another. Those bullets, aimed to harm, landed everywhere but on us. I took the weed I stole from him and transformed it to cash faster than Western Union.

Of course there just wasn't enough money in marijuana for me and I gradually started moving cocaine again. I never got caught again.

Never Going Back

For with God nothing shall be impossible. Luke 1:37

God's forgiveness is like none other. Whereas society don't want to give you a second chance or believe that you have changed, with God all things are possible. It is possible to turn your life.

The penitentiary is the closest thing to hell on Earth. It is one of the worse places an African-American man can be. Maybe the only thing worse is being an African-American man back in the general society after being incarcerated. It is hard to come out and maintain a normal lifestyle. It is hard to find people willing to give you a second chance.

When I left prison one of the guards told me, "You'll be back." I was not naïve by any means yet her words caught me by surprise. "Why would you say that?" I asked. "I've got my G.E.D." She shrugged her shoulders and said, "You didn't learn a craft, you didn't learn anything to establish a career. Those who don't go into a career field come back." Obviously she had not lived my experience and she certainly didn't know me. "I promise," I told her adamantly, "I will not be back!" She clarified her statement, "I'm not just talking about the streets I'm talking about prison boot camp. You ain't going to make it in boot camp for four months. Everybody Black that goes to boot camp comes right back. They don't make it."

"I'm going to make it through boot camp," I snapped back, "and I'm never coming back period! It's over!" She didn't understand a part of me died while I was inside. Still she continued, "You'll be back, you'll be back." Now I understand she was talking from what she had witnessed in the past. She has witnessed recidivism first hand. One study suggests that 7 out of 10 men released from prison will be back within a three year period. The rate is even higher for African-American men and unfortunately that same study suggests 16% of African-American men will go to prison in their lifetime. I'm not about to blame society for our misfortunes and mistakes, but I will say as a whole it turns it back on you once you've gone down that prison road. And here's this guard telling you what you can and can't do, will and won't do.

What's scary is that she was almost right. When I left prison I vowed to God I would turn my life around but saying it is so much easier than doing it. I got out and eventually started back selling drugs. I would land a job and after a few weeks at work someone is pulling me into the office saying they'll have to let me go because of my record, not because of my performance although I told them about my history in crime on the front end. But it will always be held over my head. When I moved to Dallas I worked at a mechanic shop and an electronics store. Both of those outings ended about two months after I started because of my past.

The jobs you are not eliminated from for having a record will usually go to someone with connections to a friend or family member of someone with an inside track. I saw a local politician Wanda Howard at a prep school game and I told her I was trying to get a program started for my church in hopes of helping out neighborhood youth. She seemed genuine and said she would be willing to help me out. She even gave me her business card and asked me to call her back. I did but she never answered her phone nor did she return my calls so I just quit calling. Had it been an election year maybe things would have been different. I don't mind hearing the word no, in fact I'd rather hear that than for someone to just blow me off.

Now some people may think if the shoe was on the other foot and I were the person with political power or an executive in some organization I would have concern with hiring or helping a person with a record. They would be dead wrong. The bible says all have sinned. We all have done something wrong and some people are still involved in mess, regardless of how spotless your record may appear. You just haven't been caught. Jesus gave us a second chance. We were all headed to hell when he gave us an opportunity to save our soul. So for a person to judge a person without even getting to know them is wrong. People still have to eat and live. But some people would rather push you back into the street and send you back to the life you are trying to get away from instead of giving you a chance.

I know what I did is wrong, but you have people treating my drug conviction as if is equivalent to murder or attempted murder. I've been off government papers for more than 15 years. Is that not long enough to start treating me like a member of the greater society? And to think, I am one of the lucky ones, but only because of my strong faith in God.

Finally Answering the Call

Moreover whom he did predestinate, them he also called: and whom he called, them he also justified: Romans 8:30a

God's providential hand of protection is always around those that he calls and predestined for His use. There may be times in your life that you don't feel worthy of His call. You may run from the call like Jonah, but anytime you run from God the only place to go is down. When His hand is on you, you may have to be imprisoned or go through trials and tribulation but He called. His call never goes unanswered. Being justified is a act of God's grace and favor.

I knew I was out of control. There is not a day that goes by that I'm not thanking the Lord I'm still living and able to share my story. There are others that are not as fortunate. A friend of mine, also name Steve, was murdered as a result of drug life back in 1992. I was just 22 at the time and some members of my crew and I had planned to go to my mom's club on this particular night but my friend Steve decided to stay back in Memphis. I had fronted him some dope about a week prior so he was planning on collecting money from someone who owed him so he could pay me back.

A few hours later while at the Red Hut I got a call from someone telling me Steve had just been killed. A group of us tried to rush out of the club destined for Memphis, but my mom was there and she locked us all in the club afraid we would pull a Dough Boy move, from the movie *Boyz 'N the Hood* and go avenge his death. She was smart to do it because we knew the guy who was said to have murdered him and we would have gone looking for him. The guy was a drug user and owed Steve money for dope Steve had given him on credit. But for whatever reason he refused to pay Steve back. Steve wasn't having any of that so Steve pulled his gun on him and walked the guy to his own house and told him to get his money. Instead the guy retrieved a knife. He and some of his family members present at his house that evening repeatedly stabbed Steve until he lost life.

If only he had decided to go with us that night things may have been different. Maybe I could have gone with him to collect the money because I was more respected on the track and Steve's death could have been avoided. This alone should have been reason enough for me to put this life style in the past. Unfortunately, it was not.

Although I was getting the money the wrong way, I was helping people out. No, this is not a blessing, but it does speak to my heart. My heart has always been good. My heart was like mother's heart. I bought my mothers' father, my granddad a duplex across the street from my mom so she could keep an eye on him. I put furniture in it, fixed it up paid his bills, bought him groceries.

People would want to be in my circle because I would do things for them, buy them all sorts of stuff. But I did stuff for people I didn't know as well. One day while in the grocery store line, this woman checking out in front of me experienced problems with her credit card, the checkout clerk couldn't get it to read. I asked her to tell me the amount of the bill. It was more than one-hundred dollars. I told her I would pay for it. She asked me for my phone number so she could repay me. I told her that would not be necessary. I admit, it felt great to be able to do that for a total stranger. Like most drug dealers, I was mentally lazy and sharing with others may have reconciled my mind for the moment, but it would do nothing for my soul.

There were so many warnings and so many signs that I should give up my wayward existence and dedicate myself to a greater cause.

I had a call from God I needed to answer but I was too busy ignoring it while satisfying my need for material things. There were signs I was meant to do more with my life and not just because I got along well with everyone nor because I was caring and compassionate. One day, during the middle of my drug selling era, my girlfriend and I were at the house preparing to leave for another trip to Mason. Someone knocked on the door. I checked to see who it was and standing on the porch was a one-legged man on crutches. I had lived in the neighborhood for years and had never seen him before. He was a blue-eyed white man with a long beard and appeared to be down on his luck. When I opened the door he just asked if I could feed him. "I'm so hungry," he said. I responded, "Sir, come on in." I hadn't been to the grocery store but before he happened upon us my girlfriend had been to KFC and we had a box of chicken sitting at the table. "You can sit at this table and eat this chicken," I told him. He replied, "Sir, God is going to bless you."

When he finished the chicken he asked if I had any coffee. I did not but I told him what I would do is give him five dollars and said, "I hope this helps." He reiterated, "God is going to bless you one day." He got up from the table, said his goodbyes and hopped out. I felt so strange at the moment. I looked at my girlfriend and said, "There's something about that man. I ain't ever seen that man in our neighborhood. Let me see which way this man went." I rushed outside to the gate of the yard, there were three houses before my mother's on the shorter end of the street I looked down and did not see him. I looked down the longer end of the road and didn't see him there either. I said to myself, there's no way this guy could have gotten this far with the assistance of a walking aid. No way.

When I told my mother and aunt about the incident they both said it was nothing but an angel from God I was entertaining. My Heavenly Father wanted to see how I would treat him. I could only hope I passed. The Bible teaches us to be careful how we treat strangers because we may be unaware that we are entertaining an angel. Funny thing is, I never saw the man again. But his imagine is a fresh photo in my mind, even to this day. I remember the white hair, the old plaid coat and the old hat. There were so many other nice people in the neighbor who would have fed him if he had stopped by their house. Instead, he picks the only house on the street at the time with a fence around it. Never did it cross my mind this man was a robber or anything like that. I just felt something about him.

Even while in the penitentiary there were signs of my calling. I was attending the church services held in prison. One night the chaplain comes from behind the pulpit and looked into the congregation of nearly 500 people. I was sitting in the back when he called out. "Young man. You with the mouth full of gold come here." Everyone started looking around and suddenly we broke out into laughter, more than half the prison population had a mouth full of gold. "You," he said pointing in my direction. "I'm talking to you." An eerie feeling came over me. "He's talking about you," one of the guys sitting near me blurted out. I felt as if the chaplain and I were the only ones in the room at that moment.

"Young man," he said. "You're about to be blessed. You are getting ready to leave here." Maybe he hadn't checked my paper work. Prison boot camp wasn't even an option for me at that time. He continued, "You're getting ready to leave here soon. God has called you to preach the gospel. I see you before a multitude of people."

The next time we congregated I decided I was going to sit elsewhere to avoid being pointed out. There was also a different chaplain so I assumed I was in luck. Nope. "Young man comes here," he said. I walked his direction thinking, "no way is this going to happen again." Wrong. He said, "I don't know you but God told me to shake your hand because you are a preacher." I replied, "No I'm not." He smiled, "you're not a preacher in here but you're getting ready to go home." Neither of these men knew me but it was the second confirmation of what my future should be.

Fast forward, and I'm out of jail and riding in my drop top Mustang kept in my mother's care while I was locked up. Riding around in Memphis I saw this woman I went to school with, so we pulled over in front of some random house, got out of our cars and started to converse about the "good ole" days. Some guy opens the door to the house steps out and yells, "Come here." My old classmate asked me if I knew him. I didn't, I figured it was time to go, people will shoot at you for a whole lot less. He could tell we were motioning toward our respective rides when he pleaded for me not to leave. "Please come here," he said. I didn't want to look like a wimp in front of a woman so I stopped to hear what he had to say. He said, "I just want to shake your hand. Either you are a preacher or are going to be one." My friend was stunned. I could hear her take a deep breath. The gentleman asked her why she reacted that way. She told him how I used to hear that all the time in school. She said I was a mini-preacher back then, albeit for anything but the right thing. "A preacher knows a preacher," He explained. "I'm a preacher and God sent me out here to shake your hand because He is about to call you into the ministry."

There is no one universal way people receive their calling from God. I had several callings. The last straw for me was the wreck I had on the interstate. It all flashed before my eyes: out of the penitentiary back to selling drugs, can't sleep at night, shooting at people, robbing Mexicans just because. All the while God kept speaking to me, telling me He did not want to send my soul to hell but I was giving Him no other choice. He kept speaking to me. I woke up many nights just sweating, walking around without a destination, and thinking about how I was going to get my life together. People could tell something was bothering me but I would not admit to it. I kept hearing God's voice tell me to "Preach the word. Preach the word." There was nothing tough to decipher from His message. His voice was distinct and clear as a mighty coronet in the still of the night. "Preach the word. Preach the word."

I didn't want to accept the responsibility the Lord was giving me but today I understand how omnipresent and ubiquitous He is and I sit in awe as His servant. "This time it will not be the penitentiary," He told me, "it will be death. I've given you ample of time to do what I've asked you to do." As a result I finally accepted my calling on New Year's night, 1997. I made a formal announcement to the church soon after. A few weeks later I preached a sermon. I decided to move to Dallas to get away from the temptations and the environment I surrounded myself with in Memphis. I was intent on not going back to drugs. Three months later I was back in Memphis and got caught up into the underworld again. I was preaching the word of God on one front and selling drugs on the other.

I never confessed to members of the church about what I was doing on the side because at the time I thought this was between God and me. I set up a defense mechanism against guilt that rationed that drugs were my way of living and as long as I was not hurting anyone, I was okay to continue. I would imagine however people suspected I was still selling drugs. I remained flamboyant with the way I dressed and the cars I drove. I even owned a beeper business and a dollar store for a spell as a cover for what I was doing. The beeper was a hot commodity during the mid-90s, but it was quickly replaced by the cell phone so that venture died. When Cricket Communications came out with their cell phones, a friend of mine asked me if I would be interested in investing in it. I was very skeptical of the company and decided not to touch it, but look at it now, not on the level of a Sprint or Verizon, but very lucrative. God is so merciful. He spoke to me again. "I've already said what would happen. My grace is sufficient."

He is so right. I rented a vehicle and apparently the guy who inspected it before I left the lot forgot to let down the hood. So as I was driving on the interstate the hood flew up blocking my vision and I ran into the wall of the highway. Another car hit me from behind. I was stunned. My adrenaline was flowing and I popped out of the car looking at the wreckage, and then looking at myself to make sure I was okay. Somehow I was not injured. People driving by stopped to make sure I was okay and upon looking at the heap of metal my car had become, they were amazed I was alive much less unscathed. I knew God saved me and he wanted me to go save others. Then a friend of mine who lived down the street was busted for selling. They had his phone bugged and some of his conversations were with me. Luckily I never said anything to incriminate myself; however, I was later told they were hoping to get a two-for-one and get me as well.

When I finally stopped selling the drugs and accepted my calling, mom was so happy. That really meant a great deal to me. She decided to sell the Red Hut club. She originally wanted me to one day take over the club and knew I would not be there to help her out or run errands had she decided to continue. Plus she said if God told me to preach, then neither she nor I would run one.

Family

But the mercy of the LORD is from everlasting to everlasting upon them that fear him, and his righteousness unto children's children; To such as keep his covenant, and to those that remember his commandments to do them. Psalms 103: 17-18

Family is a unique organism and that we didn't choose. The face of all families look different and God in his infinite wisdom didn't allow children to choose their parents. As parents, it is important to teach the precepts and principles of God. Parents make an impact on their children that can affect future generations. It is important to teach children to keep God's covenant. Psalms teaches us that the Lord's mercy is everlasting to those who keep His covenant. Although I made many mishaps in my life, my family has been there to support me and love me.

Jimmy Saine is more than 20 years older than my mother, born Earnestine McNeil. He's the very definition of old school. He has ten kids of his own and I'm close to my brothers and sisters whose blood line I share with him. The name Saine carried weight thanks to the infamous activities of my brothers and me. He was the proverbial old man living in the country with one family in one place and another family in another place. My dad is originally from Memphis, a poverty-ridden section of the city known as Foote Homes. He left there too and moved to Moscow, Tennessee as an adult. My mom was living in Somerville at the time. Together they opened a hole-in-the-wall night club/café titled the Greenville Inn. It had all the things a small town 70's club should or maybe it was taken from a western movie packed with fights, shootouts, fried chicken, and beer. "Your dad was good to me," my mom once told me of my father. "He bought me my first trailer home. He let me run the club. He's the reason's I stepped out and got my own club." Another reason she decided to run her own club is because she became tired of dad's wife and kids running up in her face being reminded that she was my father's mistress.

My father and mother never married. When he became part of my mother's life, she had two children, my brother Eddie Niles and my sister Rubystine Niles. My mother also had a son Jeffrey Niles who passed away as a baby. Together my mother and father brought four kids onto this Earth, Robin Saine (two years my senior), Sharon Saine (one year older than me), my twin sister Stephanie Saine and me. He wasn't present much, at least as far as I was concerned. Ask my sister Robin and she'll beg to differ. He loved her a lot and I believe this is because she was the first child via my mother. Robin spent her weekends with my father out in the country, along with my brother and oldest sister.

I would call him on holidays and ask for gifts. I'd ask for a bee-bee gun once to no avail. Iwanted a bike, but wouldn't get it. But, I didn't hold this against him. I can say he was there for me at times. When I got locked up in Covington, he along with all my brothers bailed me out. He died in 2000 while I was living in Dallas. My wife and I came back to the area of course to attend the funeral. Our relationship, rocky at times, improved tremendously over the years. In fact, before I moved to Texas I would go visit him and give him hundred dollar bills and things that put a smile on his face. I hoped he understood there was no animosity just love. I learned a lesson in life I hope others can benefit from and that's to treat people the way you want to be treated regardless as to how they treat you. Because of that philosophy I have no regrets as it pertains to my father. Some people waste their entire lives holding on to useless grudges and it's not until they lose a person or end up on their own death bed that they realize how senseless it all was. My father started to acknowledge me more near of his time on earth, maybe because my name was getting around since I was of course, one of the biggest dope dealers in the area.

Everyone in the country has scanners that pick up on police activities. It was a means of entertainment for some of the smaller rural towns. Some had the trunk tracking device while others used the handheld wide band receivers. People would have it playing in the background, like comfort sound, similar to leaving a television on. My father owned a scanner. At times he would hear police referencing my name on his scanners. One night while listening to the device he heard my name mentioned and rushed to the phone to call my mother and inform her I was involved in a shootout. He was afraid I had been injured or worse dead. He was really shaken up by the whole thing and was so relieved when he found out I was just fine. I knew he loved me, but with men it is so hard for us sometimes to say it. I want to make sure my children hear me say it. I want them to feel it through every fiber of their being.

I was always willing to do any and everything for my family. Even today I'm called into situations to serve as mediator. It doesn't matter what time of day it is either. It is not uncommon for me to get calls at three in the morning from people asking me to help resolve an issue. When my brother and his family moved into this new subdivision in North Memphis, his kids were subjected to harassment from this area gang called FAM. My brother called me from work and asked me to find out what was going on.

Flagrant Fouls

When I arrive at his place there were about 30 young boys just hanging around with their egos totally out of control. I may have appeared to be alone but I had God in my corner and I don't know a single gang able to beat Him down. So I said, "Ain't nobody scared of ya'll so why don't you go somewhere and sit down. Because ya'll got the right family if you want some drama. But I'm here to tell you it don't take all of that. Ya'll better get Christ in your life and leave that stupid stuff alone." I was just getting started. "You better take it from me because I've been where you all are trying to go. You are going to the graveyard or to the penitentiary."

One of the guys started circling me as if he was going to try to sucker punch me. I said, "Look young man, you need to get on away from behind me because you're gonna make me do something to you." Looking me up and down he replied, "I ain't walking behind you!" I told him like I'll tell anyone, "I pastor a church and I'm a preacher but I don't put up with any foolishness. God is still working on me. You better not do or say the wrong thing. I'm subject to click." For the most part God has helped me with my temper. Sometimes you can be nice and loving to people but they are still going to act crazy and try to push you into a corner. I just told those guys to get on. That may sound a bit harsh but it is a far cry from how I was back in the day, particularly when it pertained to my family.

When I was a big bad dealer, my cousin, also named Steve, came over my mom's house and told me some guys jumped him, robbed him and beat him up. I had the reputation of being a loose cannon, so there's no surprise he would come to me first. With watered eyes, my mom, the voice of reason as always, told me not to go over there. I was young, aggressive, and full of testosterone and wasn't hearing what she had to say. So I jumped in my car, my pleading mother got in hers, as did my stepdad, my brother and a host of others. Once we arrived we must have looked like a mob family. I got out of the car and noticed some of the guys I actually grew up with just hanging out. I had my gun out in plain view and asked my cousin to show me the perpetrator. "Point out the guys who jumped on you!" I said, loud enough for everyone to hear. One of the guys I knew intervened. "Big Steve," he called me. "Ain't nobody jumped on your cousin. He got drunk and got his ass kicked. Plain and simple." I looked at my cousin as if to ask is this true. He didn't deny it. Had he pointed someone out that night, that person would have been six feet under and I would be serving a life sentence. My mom would have probably needed therapy after watching her son end another human's life. I laid into my cousin. I thought about that scene often while I was actually locked up and thanked God it didn't end the way I intended it to when I first pulled up in my car. I thanked God mom didn't have to witness her son murder someone. This would have devastated her.

When I first started dabbling into drugs my mother was picking up clues that I was doing something and she started getting worried when I was in the eleventh grade. My lifestyle had changed and she couldn't help but notice, not just who I was hanging with but what I was spending money on. She questioned me and of course I denied dealing drugs. Like most mothers lacking evidence on their children she used the old, "I know," prosecuting method. Call it mother's intuition because she was dead on the money. But I'm 18, I'm a man now I rationed to myself and no disrespect to my mother but I had to make my own decisions. Sorry mom, yard work just wasn't cutting it any more.

I had my own place now and once I, as they called it on the streets, "picked up the sack," it was on from there. To the surprise of many this did not put a strain on my relationship with my mother. She didn't like it but she accepted it, after all I was grown and what other choice did she have? She was not going to turn me in to the authorities. I don't care how wrong you are, one thing you can always count on is the unconditional love from a mother. It's just a maternal thing, I guess. Plus, I took care of my mom. I bought her a house, a car, whatever she needed.

When I started preaching, she began to voice her concerns again. "You can't be preaching, serving the Lord and selling drugs," she told me. "You've got to do one or the other. You keep doing this you're going back to jail and that's gonna kill me because they're gonna have you locked up for a long time."

My brothers and sisters knew what I was doing also. Some of them knew too much. Rubystine, for example, once picked up $20,000 dollars for me. She did plenty of rippin' and runnin' on my behalf. One day I got a shipment of coke through the mail and didn't want to have it at my place just in case the police got word of my activities. My brother Eddie was also feeling heat in the neighborhood and suggested that I not ride with any drugs on me. I followed his advice, cooked what I had and I hid it at Ruby's house. I'll admit I was concerned that she would smoke some of my dope if she knew where it was. So I placed it in what I thought was a secure place in her bathroom. I played it slick, if not safe. I came out of the bathroom as if I still had it on my person and went to another room to give the impression I was stuffing it elsewhere.

My major concern as it pertained to her was the choices she made in raising her sons.

As for my own children I have ten, five boys and five girls. My first child was born in 1990 and also named after me. Lil' Steve, as we call him, is very bright and smart. He's currently following in my footsteps, or maybe I should say the footsteps of many Biblical heroes and is preaching. His mother, who's older than me, was youthful and wild back when I dated her and I remember when bringing Lil' Steve home as a baby and wanting to sit at home and be around him all the time. His mom would try to get me to go out with her, but I would tell her I wasn't going anywhere and needed to be home with Lil' Steve and suggested she do the same. She wasn't hearing that. She would soon gather her things, pack her bags, and jet. Fortunately for me, the bond between Lil' Steve and I grew strong over the years.

God kept Lil' Steve sheltered from the lifestyle I embraced and knew as a 20 year old. Lil' Steve avoiding the streets, gangs, drugs, is nothing short of a revelation. The young preacher has worked on his craft since the age of nine. I use to assist him with his sermons and put him up on a milk crate so he could be perfect in front of a live audience. I have some of his finished products on tape still. As he was coming of age, there were occasions where we were preaching at different churches on the same day. So while I'm running a revival in Mason, I would then have to drive to Memphis to pick him up and take him to his engagement. He still calls me from time to time for advice regarding some of his sermons. We are so close. In fact he attends church with his old man every Sunday. How many fathers can say that about their adult sons? Not many I would be willing to guess.

His mother and I both had some maturing to do back when Lil' Steve was born, but I'm proud to say the relationship between his mother and I today is stronger than ever as friends. She had three daughters when I met her, now my stepdaughters, and they would eventually begin calling me dad. Now they have children of their own and their children refer to me as granddad. In all Lil' Steve's mother and I had a total of two children together. We had one daughter after Steve.

When I did get married, it was to a woman who was about a decade younger than me. I was 31 at the time we met and initially she did not know who I was but as we began to hang out, people she knew who saw us together began to let her know who I was. She was young and accepted my drug dealing lifestyle and of course appreciated the finer things in life that came along with it. I took her all around the country, prior to that she had only been in the Memphis area. Looking back on it, I don't think she was ready for marriage. Our marriage turned sour, we went our separate ways and are now divorced.

I'm close with all ten of my children, although there are two I don't get to see as often. One child lives in Las Vegas with her mother the other is a son whose mother use to bribe me for money in exchange for seeing my own son. When my money started to come up short so did my visitation periods with my boy. I'm remaining optimistic about the entire thing. It's my prayer to bring all my kids back together. I want us to take one big family picture. I want it to be just my kids and me hanging out.

Children are a blessing, but that doesn't mean they don't come with drama. My 14-year old son, Josh, who is following Pierre's path as far as recreation goes by playing basketball with his middle school team, decides one day he wants to smack one of his female classmates and landed an eleven day suspension from school. I was so disappointed. One frustrating aspect of being a parent is trying to combat the abundance of so many outside influences

Flagrant Fouls

in a child's life. I'm sure millions upon millions of mothers and fathers in this world blame themselves for the mistakes their children make and that's not fair. True, we bare a great deal of responsibility for our kids, but we can't be with them every part of the day, every step of the way. What we can do is teach them right from wrong. We can lead by example. Still, they are going to fall short of our expectations. They are even going to fall short of their own expectations. That's life. Regardless, as we are taught through reading the Bible, spearing the rod spoils the child. When I heard about my son hitting a girl in school, the rod was in full force.

Just prior to that incident I had to get on my son after I caught him at school with dice. He said he got them from one of his classmates. I happened to know the father of the young man he was referring to so I told him I was going to call the boy's dad. Suddenly he changes his story so now I'm disciplining him for having the dice plus lying. I don't believe in just punishing or disciplining without talking to children first. It's important for them to know why they shouldn't lie or steal or hang out with a certain crowd. When you discipline a child without them understanding the reason why, you create a situation where they learn to not display certain behavior while you are around. Once they are out of their parents' presence, different story. Children need to internalize the potential consequences of their behavior and fully ingest why that particular behavior is unacceptable. They need to know we love them unconditionally, which doesn't mean they can get away with everything.

Although my children and I do not sleep under the same roof, I spend a lot of time with most of them, by picking them up from school, being around as they participate in recreational activities, and keeping them during the summer months. Yet a mother of two of my boys wants to drag me in court and tell a judge she had no idea when I last saw our sons. Please. She told a judge I'm living the plush life while residing in a big house located in the expensive side of town. She also said I'm the leader of a grandiose size church. All of this is inaccurate of course. I take it in stride because I know it is the inspired workings of the devil, which is what happens when a blessing is coming your way. You see, "when you are going through, it's to get to." All of this will be a part of my testimony when I receive my big blessing from above. Then I will look back and tell people, "You see my glory but you don't my story."

My children already know my story. Whenever I talk to them about life scenarios I try to make it as real and as vivid as possible by including my life whenever it is appropriate to do so. They know it is by the grace of God, I'm still walking this Earth, and certainly not my actions that kept me alive and safe. The Lord knows I'm sorrowful and although the flesh is weak and you are not living the way He wants you to you can't do a 180 and turn it half of the way around. You have to do a full 360 degree spin and turn it all the way around. So what I try to instill within my children is not just to do as I say but do as I now do. There is a reason I changed my ways and my children are a big part of that. They deserve the best and I'm going to continue to do what I can to make sure they get just that. I want them to see me giving respect to every person I come across, regardless of their age or profession. For me it is all about how you treat people, which brings me back to Josh.

When I asked him why he slapped his classmates he said, "She was in the lunch room with some other kids laughing at me and lying, saying I had sex with a fat girl on a swing." "Lord have mercy," I thought. "Seeds of a father." This took me back to my school days, unfortunately. When I was in the seventh grade this twelfth grade girl was talking bad about me so, ill-tempered as I was then, I retaliated by hitting her. I still have the mark where she then bit me on my eye. My son knew nothing of this story and it is crazy how things go around and come around. I told him, that's not how you handle situations. You have to be able to control your anger. I told him he has to be able to walk away and be the bigger person. You never know what is going on with people now-a-days. "What if she has brothers in a gang?" I asked him. "Or what if she had a knife or a gun when you hit her? You've got to be able to think. You can't just act on your emotions. Even when people are not treating you the way you want to be treated you still treat them the way you want to be treated." I hope he understood. I know I now understand what my mom was going through raising my siblings and me.

Pierre

And whenever you stand praying, forgive, if you have anything against anyone, so that your Father also who is in heaven may forgive you your trespasses. Mark 11:26

Forgiveness is a pill that's difficult to swallow for many people. It is important to forgive those who have wronged you. Forgiveness is not for the other person, but for you! God commands us to forgive so that we can seek forgiveness from God.

I was 17 years old June 7 1987 when my older sister Rubystine "Ruby" Niles gave birth to a baby boy. She named him Jartavious Pierre Niles. He was the younger of her two. I was happy for her, but had no idea at the time, how he would someday impact my very own life. He would grow into a massive 6-8 man-child taking on the genes of his 6-5 father Harvey Henderson. As for the name, we all called him Pierre.

My sister relied on my mom and me to babysit Pierre and his brother from time to time as she ventured into higher education. I even missed days from school at times to keep an eye on the two.

There was just something about Pierre. He became attached to me like a magnet. Once I reached my mid-to-late twenties Pierre, who was grade school age, became awe-struck at what appeared to be my glamorous life style. He saw me driving the fancy cars and wearing the fancy jewelry. If it sounds familiar it's because I did the same thing when I was his age. He was only about seven or eight, but would rush outside with a bucket and shop towel in hand ready to wash my car. He would wash it when it didn't need washing. It was a means of bonding so I would join him and we would wash it together. I would give him money for his troubles but as far as he was concerned, the payoff was being able to ride around in it with me. I enjoyed taking him shopping with me. The little things made him so happy.

I nicknamed him "P" and "Dirty Red." The "Red" part of the name came from his light reddish skin tone. I put the "Dirty" in the front because of the temper he displayed with his cousins. But with me he was different. He always wanted to prove his worth to me so in addition to washing my car, he would go and clean my room or do whatever chore he could to remain in my favor.

I hated I had to separate from him, at least physically, when I got married and moved to Dallas. We were still close as ever otherwise. He was 13 at the time. He called me asking if he could come down and stay with me for the summer. I thought to myself, "Why wait that long?" The Winter Holidays were approaching for school kids so my wife and I decided to come back to Memphis and then bring him to the big "D" with us as soon as school let out. He spent Christmas and New Year's Day with us. I brought him back home afterwards.

Seven months later, my wife and I decided to move back to Memphis. Pierre was 14 and attending Treadwell High School. Everyone could see this guy was beginning to literally grow up but for some reason I never thought much about him being a basketball player until I came back and realized how much it had become a part of his life while I was away, his first love became basketball if you will. I left Memphis thinking football was his sport of choice. I remember going out to see him play pee-wee games, rain or shine. My mom got a kick out of seeing me following and chasing him up and down the sideline encouraging him to run. Playing receiver would later help him in basketball because on the gridiron is where he developed his mobility and hand-eye coordination.

Because I was living in Texas with my wife, I did not notice things spinning out of control with my sisters' unfortunate habit until I came back to Memphis. She would drop Pierre and his brother off with my mom so she could do her thing. Most of her thing unfortunately was centered on hanging out with her crew and doing what they did. Several members of our family were fed up with it. I told her it was wrong for her to drop off her children with their grandmother at a whim with no money or food. Initially she was combative telling us to stay out of her business, although she knew she was in the wrong. One day she surprised me with a proposition. "Lil' bro, keep Pierre for me for a while, because you are right, momma's not able to do it and I need to get myself together," she said. As much as I wanted to believe her I knew she was only using me to get back to her hobby while ignoring her responsibilities.

Still I agreed after talking it over with my wife. Before I made up my mind, my sister called me at an alarming rate asking me if I had reached a decision. I finally told her my wife hadn't made it home yet but bring Pierre anyway. But she didn't just bring Pierre, she brought her oldest son, Montario also. I thought Montario would be staying with us to but as it turns out, my sister was just leaving him in my care for the night and he went back to live with my mother, his grandmother.

The very next day my sister calls with what she must have thought was a revelation of sorts. "Pierre can stay with you," she said, "but I'm taking him to Ridgeway High School." At the time, Pierre was assigned to Treadwell, which was closer to where the key member of his family resided so I objected. "Look if he's staying with me and you want me to keep him and you give me custody, you don't run my house and tell me where he's going to go school," I told her. "If I'm looking after him for you, why should that matter what school he attends if I'm feeding him, clothing him, and making sure he gets to school." That's when she dropped a series of F-bombs on me, starting with "Fuck you." That was proceeded by, "you don't tell me what to fucking do with my child." Her words and action were very contradictory. I did not understand why the need to have him in Ridgeway. She could offer me absolutely nothing.

I would later find out she was cutting a deal with his former AAU coach. His son played on the same AAU team with Pierre so he wanted to keep them paired together. It was obvious to many that with his height and all-around game, Pierre would get looks from several college coaches. As a result, his teammates would gain access to these coaches by default.

Pierre didn't even want to go. When Ruby came by my house to pick him up, Pierre, fighting back tears, was adamant in his position, telling her he preferred to stay with me. "I'm your mom!" she snapped. "You listen to me! You're going with me."

While he was gathering his things he told me his mom was going to make him stay with his AAU coach. But it's my sister's child. I wasn't going to argue with her. I could only make a suggestion and move on. She also got her wishes and enrolled him at Ridgeway High School.

Two weeks later my mother called and me Ruby and Pierre were having constant shouting matches. She said Pierre left the house walking. She told me which direction he was headed and asked me to pick him up. Memphis doesn't stay cold long, but during the short period when the temperatures actually drop in the Bluff City, it can be nearly unbearable and Pierre just happened to pick one of those days to decide to "walk" away from home. I raced to my truck to look for him and lucky spotted him making his pilgrimage to nowhere in particular. I pulled up to him, "P, what's going on?" I could tell he was flustered. "I'm sick of her," he said. "She ain't got no food in the house and we ain't got nothing to eat. She stole my money." My heart dropped. I knew my sister was not the most responsible person at the time but this was hard to swallow. How could she not provide him with even the basic human needs? "Just come on," I told him. "You're coming with me."

The conversation turned even more serious when I told him of my plan. "This is what we're going to have to do. We've got to go down to juvenile court. We've got to get this documented." I thought this was a necessary procedure because when Ruby found

Flagrant Fouls

out he was with me, she threatened to get the police involved.

She threatened to tell the authorities that I was a robber and a drug dealer. There was no real merit behind her claims. My robbing and drug selling days were behind me. It was getting personal. True to her word the police were knocking at my door about an hour later. When I opened the door her words she unleashed the remaining F-bombs she had stored in her arsenal. The police officer had to intervene and ask her to calm down so he could hear what I had to say. If looks could kill my sister would have been charged with murdering me as I tried to explain my side of things to the officer.

While I was talking to the policeman my mother pulled up. She told the officer she was not interested in taking sides but needed to set the record straight. "These two are both of my children," she told him. "She asked him to keep her son. When he kept him, when he brought him in his house, she came back after she changed her mind because he told her he would not let her run his household and she got mad about that so she came and got him. But he doesn't want to be with his mom now because there's a lot of stuff going on that I'm not going to share with you at this point, but she's wrong to have you come to his house like he's done something."

So the police officer took a diplomatic approach and asked Pierre who he would prefer to stay with until the matter was resolved in court. Pierre didn't hesitate, "My uncle." The policeman said he believed

Pierre was old enough do decide on his own so he let him stay with me. My sister didn't take this news in stride, and began another F-bomb assault. Some of them targeted at me while the others were aimed at the police officer, who had to threaten to put her in the back of the squad car to shut her up. "You'll be hearing from my lawyer!" Ruby told me. So I realize I knew I better invest in one myself.

It is a shame we had to resolve the situation in a court of law but for a little more than two months, we were in and out the courthouse. We both let the judge listen to our character witnesses. Then suddenly, before the judge could share his opinion, my sister asked if she could speak. This time she issued an assault on my morals. "My brother," she told the judge, "he doesn't need Pierre. He just wants him for his money and what he's going to become, because he's got a future in basketball." The judge interrupted her. "He's only 14," he said. "How does he know what he's going to become? He's not God."

So members of my family took the witness stand, including my mother and brother, all testifying how active I was in Pierre's life before he even entertained the idea of playing basketball. When I got on the stand the judge asked me if I loved my nephew. "Of course," I answered. Then he asked if I was capable of taking care of him, provide for him, and feed him. "Yes sir," I replied. I then added, "I don't have to get custody of him. I have kids of my own. I have to take care of them so I don't need another mouth to feed.

But I will be very upset if the court gives him back to her because she's unfit."

My mother told the judge I was the only person Pierre would listen to. He carefully considered all that he'd heard over the days and decided to take a break before sharing his opinion. During this brief intermission he spoke with my sister. I have no idea what they spoke about but as I waited in the hallway my sister came up to me and told me she loved me and she no longer wanted to keep this infighting in the family going. "You can keep him," she said. Maybe the judge told her he would grant me custody and this was her way of not losing, but instead conceding. Regardless the judge acknowledged Pierre's poor quality of life under her care and reasoned that since I, of all of Pierre's family members, was the only one interested in taking him in and the fact he wanted to be with me, he said it was the court's decision to award custody of Pierre to me.

When I gained custody of Pierre, I made it clear he had to abide by my rules. He had to come in when I said come in. I love him and I let him know he wasn't going to be out shooting craps, smoking weed, or coming into the house at any time he got ready. I told him he would have household responsibilities like taking out the garbage. As far as I was concerned he was a child in need of discipline. I knew people would let him get away with certain things because he was an upcoming prospect, but I would not be one of them.

My concern was with my nephew and my mother. I wanted him to be in a better environment and given a chance to succeed in life. The problem with my sister is that she wanted to be a part-time parent. She didn't want the responsibility of raising a child, but she wanted to tell me how to raise one.

During this time, I had no idea about Pierre being on anyone's radar basketball wise I was just a concerned uncle who didn't want to see his nephew on the streets and it appeared as if no one could handle him but me. Pierre had a bit of temper and could be intimidating to people, including adults, with his baritone voice and towering stature.

Perhaps the worst part of the ordeal was Pierre knowing of his mother's issues. Of course we spoke about it on several occasions. One day he called me crying. A couple of days prior I had given him several pairs of my old basketball shoes. I'd owned so many that I'd only worn most of them a few times. In one of the sneakers I forgot I left a wad of cash. It was chump change to me at the time. I kept all my big money in the closets behind the wall, the fifty and hundred dollar bills. He was talking so fast and so upset when he called that I could barely understand him. "I found your money and Ruby took your money," he said. "You had a whole lot of money in your shoe, a whole lot of ones, fives, and tens. She's gonna take that money and go spend it on something unnecessary."

I think knowing really hurt him, more so as he grew older. People in the neighborhood knew his mom had a problem although you could not tell just by just looking at her.

My relationship with Ruby hit an all-time low when she told me once she wanted me dead. She claimed the devil ordered her to kill me. God wouldn't let her touch me because as I said before, he had a bigger plan for me. My sister, it seems had a different plan. This is something you would expect from some of the people I use to deal with out on the streets, but not with my very own sister. She even threatened to plant drugs in my car and get me busted. She had developed a genuine hatred for me. This hate was rooted in me having custody of Pierre. She didn't appreciate the perception in the community of not being able to take care of her own son.

My mother had custody of my sister Robin's boys. So believe me, Ruby was well aware of what people were saying behind Robin's back. She even had Pierre's dad, who had never been a part of his life to that point, following me around trying to catch me doing something illegal so she could get Pierre back. I was not about to jeopardize my life and freedom any more. I had too much to look forward to with me preaching and having custody of Pierre. No way.

Our frosty relationship even split the family down the pro-Steve, and pro-Ruby line. She would stop at no lengths to defame my name and character to members of my family. It took years for some of them to understand the whole truth, and the whole truth is, it's not just about my nephew, it's about my family and I want to be there for them just as my mom has set the example by always being there for us.

I'm glad to say today my relationship with Ruby is much better. Much of the credit for rebuilding the relationship goes to my mother, who consistently stayed on us about working out our differences. Like I said before, my mother had always been the rock in our family.

Although Pierre's relationship with his dad has improved slightly (as a result Pierre added his father's last name "Henderson" and now goes by Pierre Henderson-Niles), his relationship with his mother is still a work in progress. They talk on the phone from time to time because she currently lives in Toledo, Ohio, which of course makes it tough to communicate face to face. At some point they will have to open the communication lines and have an honest discussion about what has transpired in the past. Asking either one to forget the hardships is impossible, but hopefully somewhere in their hearts is a place to for forgiveness. Only then will they be able to move forward.

Prelude to a Deal

For what shall it profit a man, if he shall gain the whole world, and lose his own soul? Mark 8:36

At the end of this life, riches and fame will diminish. In the end, it will not matter what ambitious goals, riches or wealth you've obtained. None of these things can be taken with you when this life is over. Worldly desires will be lost but only what you do for Christ will ultimately transcend this world into life everlasting. You will be judged by a just God who has died so that you don't have to die with no hope.

When I was granted custody of Pierre, my wife and I took him out of Ridgeway and sent him back to Treadwell. I was happy with Pierre attending Treadwell and despite his mother's wishes for him to attend Ridgeway there was nothing she could say or do to make me change my mind. But there was something Pierre would do. He really wanted to be at Ridgeway and he told me this. He had made some good friends during his short time at Ridgeway. In addition, some of his AAU teammates played there and people in that particular school district were not privy to knowledge about his mother's drug habit. Plus, I knew it had a solid reputation of being a good academic institution. So I talked it over with my wife and we decided to move to an area which would put us in the Ridgeway School district. Once we got him enrolled he really liked the school and flourished under Coach Wes Henning on the basketball court. Being around people he was familiar with provided Pierre with a certain degree of comfort. This would later factor into his decision to attend the University of Memphis and become a Tiger.

I, like most people born and raised in Memphis, grew up a fan of Memphis Tigers' basketball or as we called it before the University changed the name in the mid-'90s, Memphis State. After the coach Dana Kirk scandal in mid-'80s the school hired Larry Finch to replace him and at least from an ethical perspective, my Tigers had a model program.

Today I wonder if I should feel sorry for former Memphis Athletics Director Robert C. Johnson or should he be to blame? In fairness, he's been taking heat since he arrived at the University of Memphis. Until the time he persuaded Calipari to come to Memphis back in 2000 he was only known around town as the guy who pushed Finch out of coaching at Memphis. However, this was not the case. Finch, who is considered Memphis' favorite son, once said he knew Johnson was only the trigger man and the university's president at the time, V. Lane Rollins ordered the job. Still, typically it's the responsibility of the athletics director to make those tough decisions. Thus Johnson became infamous for his role in Finch's firing.

Perhaps the only thing worse, public relationship wise, than getting rid of Finch was finding his replacement. Memphis is a very race conscious city and at the time, U of M basketball was the only local sports program that could get people emotionally charged. Although the top brass at the University of Memphis will never admit it, they probably felt a little pressure to replace Finch, the first African-American Head Basketball Coach at Memphis, with another African-American. That's the only way I could understand the hiring of Tic Price, a coach at New Orleans. The hiring, as it would turn out, was a catastrophe. Early into his third year as coach, Price, a married man, was terminated after his affair with a student at the university surfaced. Strike two. Johnson, now needed to hit a home run. With bat in hand he was ready to swing. What did he have to lose?

Johnny Jones, a solid coach who performed admirable on an interim basis when Price was asked to leave, thought the '99-'00 season was his audition for a permanent position. He had a reputation as one of the best assistant coaches in the nation and here was his opportunity to prove he could be the lead man. Johnson, however, was looking for someone with more experience and a more dynamic personality. But Calipari? Why would he want to leave his job as an assistant with the Philadelphia 76ers, who were in the middle of a serious playoff run, to coach in Memphis? Surely he was just bidding his time while waiting his turn for another shot with an NBA team after being fired by the Nets.

Apparently Johnson knew better. I guess he realized that Calipari was done with the NBA and was waiting for the perfect college opportunity. What's perfect about coaching in Memphis? 1) It's not the NBA. Face it, the Association is a players' league. Think about it, as brilliant as Phil Jackson has been during his coaching career, if a team owner had to choose between Jackson and Michael Jordan, he/she would pick Jordan. There is no such thing as franchise players on the college level. If a player is among the elite in college, there's a great chance he will only be with the program for a season or two. Good coaches become the cornerstone of a schools' athletic program. The constant at Duke has been Mike Krzyzewski, at Syracuse it's Jim Boeheim, at Indiana it was Bobby Knight. Johnson wanted that at Memphis. 2) Calipari could be at a place where he could get what he wanted. In his autobiography, *Refuse to Loose*, Calipari talked about how he needed to change the environment when he took the job at UMass. His favorite word became, "unacceptable." He used it often when dealing with the university's administrators. He demanded things for his program and players that other teams in the Atlantic 10 had. Cal reasoned if he was going to be competitive in terms of recruiting and winning games, he needed equal footing or as close to equal as possible. 3) Like Johnson, what did Calipari have to lose? In the Tigers previous four seasons before Calipari took over, the Tigers were 16-15, 17-12, 13-15, and 15-16 respectively.

Poor Johnny Jones. Johnson continued to say publicly Jones was a candidate for the coaching job when in actuality, it was Calipari's for the taking. With Jones as interim coach, the Tigers were host of the Conference USA Tournament. No one figured they stood much of a chance of winning it, yet it was their only hope of getting into the NCAA Tournament. The Tigers won their first game against the University of South Florida, 60-58. Then the tournament's top seed Cincinnati suffered a serious blow when their All-America player Kenyon Martin broke his leg. The tournament was up for grabs at that point but as the coaching cliché' goes, you have to take it one game at a time and the next game for the Tigers was against DePaul. What if? What if they could beat DePaul? What if they could make it all the way to the tournament final game? What if they could win it and get an automatic bid to the Big Dance? What if they could win a game in the tournament? What would that say about Jones coaching ability? How would it effect Johnson's decision? Of course he had all but moved Calipari into his new office on the Memphis campus. We can only wonder because the Tigers lost to DePaul,

80-76.

Calipari walked into the Pyramid at the end of the conference tournament flanked by Johnson and a host of the U of M media relations staff. The university was making it official, Calipari was their man. Johnson gleamed. Cal was at his best. He obviously had done his homework. He rattled off names of people in the Memphis basketball community as if he'd known them for years. He was humble and warned fans it wouldn't be easy. He talked about how the team needed the support of the community. He said he would seek advice from Finch. No doubt an A+ from a public relations standpoint. I admit, knowing what happened at UMass, I had my suspicions. The Minutemen had to forfeit their Final Four appearance when it was discovered that their star player Marcus Camby had received gifts from an agent while in college. Calipari was never implicated in the incident yet it looked a bit odd when he left to coach the NBA soon after the Camby ordeal came to light. Still, I was a fan of Memphis basketball since I was a kid and I was willing to give him the benefit of the doubt.

In his first season, Calipari led the Tigers to the NIT Final Four. They lost to Tulsa, 72-64 in a semifinal game. His first season did not go without incident. Several patterns during his tenure at Memphis would start that season, actually before it. Two of the area's best players, Raleigh-Egypt's duo shooting guard Scooter McFadgon and small forward Lou Wright signed with U of M before Calipari was named the coach. When he was hired Calipari made it his business to check out the two who were in the middle of their post season. Although I never heard this from Calipari himself, the word is he was not impressed, although the two were heralded players nationally. If that's true, Wright must have done Cal a favor when he failed to meet academic qualifications to get into the University, meaning Calipari did not have to sign him while at the same time would have deal with the public's ire for not inking a local kid.

McFadgon, it appeared, was a blessing for coach. During his freshman year Calipari inserted him into the starting line-up ahead of another local player, senior Marcus Moody. Although Moody was a better scorer than McFadgon, the freshman was Calipari's kind of player. He didn't talk back to him and he did what was asked of him. Senior Shyrone Chatman was of the same mode. Chatman, who was used as a shooting guard under the previous regime, was converted to a point guard under Calipari. He seemed to flourish under the role. Moody, meanwhile, was the odd man out. He did not particularly care for how he was being utilized and quit the team. He later asked to rejoin the Tigers and Calipari made him face his teammates first. That same season another Memphis player, John Grice from Central High School and a guy from New Orleans named Courtney Trask were suspended indefinitely for violating team rules.

McFadgon, who seemed to regress during his sophomore season with the addition of one-and-done Dajuan Wagner, asked to be released from his scholarship after his second season. Calipari was surprised by the request. McFadgon's mom Cathy Sweargen attended the meeting. McFadgon and his family did not have anything negative to say about Calipari but privately felt Cal put McFadgon on the back burner. Calipari did not want to lose McFadgon of course, he was his kind of player, and he told McFadgon's mom, assuming her job with FedEx was somehow connected with the U of M that he wasn't sure how her decision would affect her future with the corporation. She informed Calipari that she had been with the company before her son was even born.

Incidents like these early in his coaching tenure at Memphis and one could see how Calipari would come to the conclusion that coaching players in their own backyard could be a difficult task at time. If not for the fact that he was one of college's premiere recruiters nationally, his stay in Memphis would be full of headaches with all the local talent in the area. Because he was able to pull some of the best kids

Flagrant Fouls

from everywhere, he didn't have to rely on local recruits. This was very important because fair or not, true or untrue, he has never had a reputation of being a great x's and o's guy. So how did he become this great recruiter? In time, I would find out first hand. In the meantime, Calipari would begin constructing his dynasty at the University of Memphis and Johnson could relax for the moment.

Striking a Deal

And the devil, taking him up into an high mountain, shewed unto him all the kingdoms of the world in a moment of time. And the devil said unto him, All this power will I give thee, and the glory of them: for that is delivered unto me; and to whomsoever I will I give it. If thou therefore wilt worship me, all shall be thine. Luke 4: 5 - 7

In my quest to stop living one lifestyle, the devil lured me into another one that gave people a false sense of power over me. They provided me a way to secure my future without selling drugs. I could care for my family in what I saw as a legitimate manner. However, I wasn't relying on God. In all we do, we must worship God and Him alone we have to serve. He is able to provide and with his provisions there is no sorrow.

Calipari told of an amusing story in his autobiography about how he was able to land Marcus Camby while at UMass. Camby, a seven-foot agile big man was a rare talent. He was a good passer, a solid rebounder, a great shot blocker, and a developing post player. One problem, he wanted to handle the rock and play guard. Knowing Camby could in essence pick any college, Calipari said he agreed to let Camby play guard but informed him that at Massachusetts they play their guards in the post. I don't know if he said this tongue and cheek or not, but it's revealing as to the level Calipari was willing to go to make sure he got who he wanted.

It did not take long for Cal to work his magic at Memphis either. Calipari's most important player from his first recruiting class at Memphis wasn't John Grice, Scooter McFadgon, or Modibo Diarra it was a player who was not heavily recruited, at least not for his playing ability; not that he was a bad player. Arthur Barclay, a six-eight power forward from Camden, New Jersey had a very charismatic personality and a career at Memphis that was more defined about what he did off the court than on it. When his eligibility ran out Calipari would brag about how Barclay received his diploma and about his white collar job working at FedEx. Calipari would say Barclay was prepared for L-A-B or life after basketball. Barclay bought into Calipari's vision. "Watch out," he once said, "Calipari is building a dynasty (in Memphis)." Bad knees limited his impact on the court but he was never lacking for effort or leadership. Once Barclay, tired of teammate Sean Banks' whining and complaining, decked him in eye causing Banks to sport a shiner for a couple of games. But more than an enforcer and a leader, Barclay had a quality like no one else; he was best friends with another player out of the Camden area, Dajuan Wagner.

Dajuan, the son of 80's Louisville sharp shooter Milt Wagner, was a grade below Barclay and pledged to attend whatever college his best friend Barclay attended. Wagner was not just a good player, he was outstanding. During his senior year he showcased his talent in Memphis when his high school team travelled to the city to take on Hamilton High. Wagner's Camden team won 78-63. Despite Hamilton's coach Ted Anderson scolding his team during time outs about letting "one man beat you," Wagner scored 50 points. More impressive than that, Wagner torched some poor team that same year for 100 points. He was named the 2001 Naismith Prep Player of the Year and averaged 42.5 points a game his senior season. Many speculated he would go straight to the pros out of high school.

Shortly after Barclay declared his intentions to attend Memphis, Dejuan's dad Milt joined Calipari's staff as Coordinator of Basketball Operations. Dajuan would follow suit and attend Memphis the next year. To justify Barclay joining the team, Calipari pointed to him as being part of a state champion at Camden and being selected to play in the prestigious Louisville Derby game. Milt, he said, was a champion. He talked about how the older Wagner had won on every level, including a championship while at Louisville and as a member of the Lakers in the NBA. Calipari pulled this off with the world watching.

In the years to come, he would continue to use the buddy system to his advantage. One of the most coveted recruits from the high school class of 2003 was a 6-10 center from Ozen High School in Beaumont, Texas named Kendrick Perkins. Keena Young was Perkins' teammate at Beaumont and a three-time all-region and all-state player. Good player, but no Perkins. Yet, Perkins and Young were good friends and were both offered scholarships to play at Memphis. Both players committed to do just that initially but Perkins did a 180 and decided to enter his name in the NBA Draft. And wouldn't you know it, suddenly apparently Young's stock dropped, at least as far as Calipari was concerned and he pulled his scholarship offer to Young. He did this too with the world watching.

In 2008, Cal signed Tyreke Evans to a scholarship. Evans' personal trainer Lamont Peterson joined his staff shortly after as a personal assistant. Calipari explained he did not have an opening on his staff when Evans signed and only considered him when a job became available. Again he was bold enough to do this with the world watching and apparently the NCAA as well. In January 2010, the chief governing body for college athletics approved a rule to prohibit programs from hiring any person associated with a recruit within a two-year radius of the athlete enrolling at the school. The ruling awaits the approval of the NCAA Board of Directors. In an awkward moment for the university, R.C. Johnson was interviewed on ESPN's "Outside the Lines" about the ethics of so-called "package deals." He backed his coach and said he didn't see anything wrong with them. And Johnson said this with the world watching.

By the time Evans arrived on campus, I was totally hip to the ways of Calipari. I was knee deep into one of his schemes myself. While travelling on the AAU circuit with Pierre I became acquainted with several of the "players" in the recruiting game. Calipari had always talked about how he liked that so many people within the Tigers' fan base believe they have ownership in the team and that they make a difference in the team's success. Well sometimes these players REALLY can make a big difference.

Travis King is one of those players. Back when Amare' Stoudemire committed to play at U of M, he and his younger brother Marwan were living with King for a little more than a year. Home Box Office (HBO) accused King of trying to use Stoudemire to obtain a coaching job. Suspicions arose when Stoudemire decided to attend an Adidas sponsored camp which King coached. And because King was pals with Calipari, Stoudemire's decision to attend Memphis became a target of interest as well. Stoudemire, of course, never attended U of M, electing to declare for the NBA Draft instead and eventually cutting ties with King.

Flagrant Fouls

Still King was an advocate for the University of Memphis. He was a very likable guy with a tough demeanor. I will say this about King, he was always up front and honest with me. In addition to Calipari and Memphis coaching staff, King was a major recruiter for the University.

"They really want Pierre," King shared with me during an AAU Tournament. He told me how arrangements were made for Shawne Williams, who was one-and-done at Memphis the year before Pierre arrived, received a SUV as an incentive to become a Tiger. He asked of me, "What would it take for Pierre to come?" I told him Pierre was already interested in attending Memphis anyway. "Still, let 'em help you," he said. King knew I was unemployed at the time and said, "You need a job right? Let 'em help you." I decided to take him up on this offer. He said he would look into it and talk to some people.

Calipari really seemed intent on getting Pierre to Memphis. He would come out to AAU tournaments all across the country to make sure Pierre saw him in attendance. Cal perceived competition though. Pierre was receiving several calls, letters, and scholarship offers from schools everywhere. Tennessee's new coach Bruce Pearl appeared to want him in Knoxville just as bad as Calipari did. During down time at one of the AAU events, Pierre and I were relaxing in our hotel room when Calipari called, as I was on the phone with him Pearl comes knocking on the door. Cal could hear him in the background. "You tell that ugly orange suit wearing mutha fucker to take his ass back to Knoxville," Cal quipped. When I hung up the phone with Calipari I told Pearl who I had been on the phone with and he had some choice words for Calipari as well. And to think all the feuding that people think exists between the two of them actually does. I would gather that most of it stems from recruiting the same players and competing in the same state.

The next time I saw King he had a bit of bad news. "They" would not be able to get me a job he informed me. I'm not sure if this had something to do with my record as if it were something else, regardless, that avenue was closed. However, "they" were willing to do something. "Man, take it," King said. "They helped Shawne." When he said this it reminded me of something Shawne said a year or two prior while on the AAU circuit. "I ain't going to Memphis unless they give me some money." Those were his words. Whether he received a dime or a vehicle from Memphis I do not know for sure, but I do know what happened with Pierre and I.

I reiterated to King when he came back to me that Pierre wants to attend Memphis. He replied, "They don't know that. So what will it take, will $1,300 do?" If I can't get a job I told him, then I'd want to at least cover my bills. I estimated that to be about $2,000 a month. When King came back he said they could only do $1,500. The first two times I received payments from King it was in that amount. I thought nothing of it at the time but I decided to meet Calipari's assistant, Derek Kellogg (D.K) myself and he gave me two grand. Of course I wondered about why the $500 dollar difference, but I pressed on. The payments had begun during the summer before Pierre's senior year in high school.

I never felt awkward when D.K. and I would have our little monthly gatherings. I had gotten used to him on the AAU scene. He would come drop in on Pierre and me while we were in our hotel rooms. My relationship with D.K. developed during the recruiting process. He became more comfortable with me and I became more comfortable with him. The feeling of trust was mutual. I felt like I had the upper hand in this situation because they were the ones persistent in their pursuit of Pierre.

The deal I struck with Cal's crew was $2,000 for five years. "They" suggested the five year period. I thought five was an odd number since Pierre would be there no longer than four years if that. If the NBA had not implemented a rule stating a person needed to be one year removed from high school to enter the draft, Pierre may have made the jump from twelfth grade to the pros. So I had my suspicions that maybe it was Cal's intention to red-shirt him a season and hold him there an extra year for some reason.

Maybe he thought keeping Pierre around would help stabilize the middle because it was hard to find and get a quality post player on the team, with guys like Stoudemire, Qyntel Woods (who also played in the NBA), and Kendrick Perkins committing but never stepping foot on campus. Who really knows?

What was defined was our deal, which could conjure up memories of Memphian and Trezevant High School football player Albert Means signing to play at Alabama with his coach Lynn Lang as his unofficial advisor. Means and his family claimed at the time they knew nothing of Lang receiving kickbacks from booster Logan Young to steer Means to the Crimson Tide. A report would later dispute this claim; regardless I let Pierre in on everything that was going on. A good portion of the money I was getting was going to him anyway.

D.K. was Calipari's right hand man and he was the only person I ever dealt with regarding money issues. No one would ever be around when he handed me the money, which was always cash payment.

Now I did get the feeling the basketball secretary may have suspected something with me requesting to see Kellogg around the same time every month.

As time progressed D.K. and I would make the exchange at various locations. In addition to the University of Memphis' Athletics Office Building, we would make the transaction on other on-campus sites, like the Larry O. Finch Center.

Sometimes I would go into D.K.'s office and he would act as if he was packing or doing something and would greet me with "What's up Man?" which would be accompanied by a $2,000 handshake.

Sometimes the exchange would be in the hallway of the office near the stairway, and sometimes we did business in the parking lot while he was on the phone with me. "Where you at?" he asked. "I'm pulling up," I would say. When I arrived he would slide me an envelope, I would put it in my coat without turning off my car, not even putting it in neutral and then keep moving once I received the funds.

Once we met in the men's restroom at the Finch Center like a mob movie. We met before at TGI Friday's downtown. I remember one meeting at his apartment downtown with him on the phone with his fiancée. He held his hand over the mouthpiece of the phone and whispered to me, "One moment, I'm talking to my fiancée." Then he got off the phone saying, "Uncle Stevie is here, we're trying to tighten something up on Pierre." This I guess was his way of throwing her off the scent.

For two straight seasons during the Conference USA Tournament, he was late with the payment, but made arrangements to meet me at the hotel the team was staying in. The money was always in an envelope, always hundred dollar bills.

The University also made arrangements with me to have dental work through Memphis Athletics Ministries Founder and Executive Director, Ken Bennett. The organization has been helping poor children in one of the poorest sections in Downtown Memphis since 1987. But I had never met Ken until Pierre began playing with the Tigers. The idea for me to have the dental work done came at the suggestion of D.K. who said, in a gentle manner, the gold "grill" decorating my teeth were not becoming of me. I understood what he was saying. Calipari didn't like his players wearing ear rings or decorative metal in their mouths. In fact, part of the terms of playing for the Tigers, former guard Antonio Burks, had to have his grill removed. So I understood, I didn't want to be the cause of any friction between the team and Pierre so I obliged. Again, D.K. said the expenses would be taken care of and put me in contract with Bennett. As it happens, Bennett received a lot of credit for getting Burks and later Andre Allen, both of whom attended Booker T. Washington High School in Memphis, into the University of Memphis. He was also responsible for making the arrangements with the dental group for me to have my custom gold removed from my mouth.

Toward the end of my dealings with D.K. before he left to coach where Calipari made his name, UMass, things started to get a little unpredictable. He brought me $1,500 on three different occasions, saying he would get the other $500 to me later. It reminded me of what happened earlier with Travis King. Eventually D.K. tried to hook me up with some guy in California and get me to go door to door selling basketball paraphernalia as a cover up. I thought to myself, "You're kidding me right?" That's not a job, and it's certainly not an adventure. I was much too old for that at the time, but that would have been their way, I guess, for justifying the money should it ever come up or either keep from paying me the money.

I wanted to make sure Pierre and I were not left out in the cold before D.K. left for UMass. Rumors had begun circulating that he was looking to move on even before the job became available so I spoke with King about how D.K. began to slack on either paying me on time or making full payments. I didn't know what was going on. I told him if "they" were interested in trying to make it look legit "they" could help me get my phone accessories store started back up. The word got back to D.K. and he asked me what it would take to get my store started back up. I told him $40-50 grand, figuring "they" would go for the lowball number of $40,000. "I'll go talk to coach," he said, "and see what "they" are saying. But I don't think they're willing to go that deep but they're willing to get close to it." So I waited. In the meantime "they" resumed with the regular payment plan as I awaited word on what would happen with the big payment.

When D.K. finally reported back to me, he told me "they" would only be able to do $35,000. "It needs to be close to $50,000," I said. "They can at least come up with $40,000." Let the negotiating continue. "I'll go back and see what 'they' say," he said. The next time I saw him the number had dropped significantly. "It's getting crucial," he said. "They are only going to be able to do $20,000." He brought me four payments of $5,000 over a two month span. D.K. was slick about what he was doing, so I had to wonder if he was getting a cut of the money. Obviously I had no proof. I couldn't go to Cal. He was smart enough to keep his hands clean. Those were the final payments and I'm sure they were happy to have me out of their hair in that regard, but at the same time not pleased I had begun to look at other places to send Pierre, not because of the money, but because he was not happy at the U of M. I made phone calls to Bruce Pearl at Tennessee and Scott Edgar at Southeast Missouri about Pierre transferring. They both seemed receptive, but the decision was up to Pierre.

Promises

It was for freedom that Christ set us free; therefore keep standing firm and do not be subject again to a yoke of slavery. Galatians 5:1

Remember that freedom has been purchased for all on Calvary's cross. Jesus Christ has paved the way for our freedom and for us to live a life of freedom. A person should never bow down to bondage of promises, position, or situations. Broken promises can lead to bondage beholding to another person who can only give you temporary satisfaction or position. All freedom is found in Christ and don't allow others to tie you down or enslave you.

I'll take Memphis basketball talent over any city on this Earth. Former Memphis basketball coach, the late Dana Kirk use to brag about how he could get in his car and go on a recruiting trip with a full tank of gas. There were some great players to play at the University that were from Memphis or cities and towns like West Memphis just next to it. Larry Finch, Keith Lee, William Bedford, Andre Turner, Penny Hardaway, Lorenzen Wright, Cedric Henderson, Elliot Perry, all household names in Memphis and all played at the University.

Funny, it is said one of the reasons Larry Finch lost his job as the head coach at the U of M was because he began losing out on the top tier local recruits. Guys like Tony Harris, who played at UT, and Robert O'Kelly, who signed with Wake Forest. Yet John Calipari did not appear to be big on recruiting inside out but more outside in. I'm not criticizing his strategy, but it was certainly a change. He appeared to nab the less heavily recruited players like Jeremy Hunt and Andre Allen, although both ended up being good players for the University. I was actually pleasantly surprised he was interested in my nephew, Pierre. Although Calipari didn't know it, this would be his easiest recruit to land. Joe Jackson, the point guard out of White Station High School in Memphis that current coach Josh Pastner would sign, is the latest version of Pierre in terms of recruiting. Joe and Pierre both knew all along they wanted to attend the University of Memphis. Still you have to play the game. You know, let them think you are interested in other schools to see how bad they really want you...how serious they are about you. Find out how they plan to work you into the future of their program. This is all important stuff these days.

According to Travis King, Cal's real motivation of getting Pierre to the U of M was to quiet some of the locals. Cal had lost area guys like Wayne Chism, who signed with Tennessee, and couldn't afford lose out on many others.

High school kids will commit to schools only to change their minds a few months later and coaches will pull scholarship offers from students should they feel the need to. It is a tough situation for both sides. A coach could be close to signing a kid who is a consensus top 10 recruit in the nation. Yet because he has only one remaining scholarship to give and is really in need of someone for a particular position, he may sign another guy who is not as talented as the top 10 recruit, but is a solid player and willing to commit. So what happens when the top 10 recruit finally decides he wants to play at the school? Think about that because it happens.

Pierre was fortunate because he wanted to be at the University and Calipari, it appeared wanted him there. Once we had the monetary situation squared away there was still a problem, Pierre's grades. Calipari came to me after we made the deal concerned about it. Of course I was aware of Pierre's academic situation. He was not failing school, yet he was at risk of failing to meet the academic qualifications at the University of Memphis. Cal and D.K. had both met with Ridgeway's head coach Wes Henning and came to me frustrated at what they thought was a lack of effort on Henning's part to help maintain Pierre's academic standings. They said Henning was only concerned with using Pierre to win state titles. Calipari suggested Pierre attend a prep school.

Traditionally prep schools are designed to prepare students for the challenges of college. They can be very expensive, especially for your average middle class working family. Somewhere, somehow, several prep schools started popping up across America with an emphasis on sports, basketball in particular. In February, 2006 the New York Times writer Pete Thamel wrote a lengthy article on the ills of these so-called prep schools. Essentially the article suggested they were places to manufacture and refine young men into better basketball players while giving the appearance to outsiders that the focus is more about education. There were huge problems at these types of schools often referred to as diploma mills. In fact, in 2007, the NCAA initiated an investigation into several of the schools including Laurinburg Institute, located in Laurinburg, North Carolina. After their review, the NCAA concluded that member institutions would no longer be allowed to accept grades and diplomas from the school and some others like it. Oddly enough, the school was once a proud school for Black students started in the early 1900s with the intent on giving African-Americans a fair shot at gaining an education. Somewhere through the years it became noted for producing amazing basketball talent, which included high school legend Earl "The Goat" Manigault, instead of academic scholars.

During the 2004-2005 college basketball season, prior to the NCAA's ruling on prep schools, Laurinburg Prep put together an amazing squad whose starting five included Shawne Williams, Robert Dozier, Antonio Anderson, Kareem Cooper, and Roburt Sallie. All of those players with the exception of Sallie were members of the Memphis '05 recruiting class, maybe the best class ever at the University of Memphis. Sallie would join three years later. That Laurinburg team finished the season 40-0 which concluded with a prep school national title. However the things happening behind the scenes of this prep school and others did not register to me at the time when Calipari suggested I send Pierre. My major concern was making sure Pierre was able to get caught up and qualified to attend the University of Memphis so I spoke to Pierre about it and we agreed it was for the best. The decision came with school already in session and Pierre enrolled at Ridgeway for his senior year. As you might expect, Coach Henning was not too pleased with this decision. His relationship with Calipari deteriorated from that point on.

It all happened so fast. Within a day or two of the decision Pierre was off to Charlotte Harbor, Florida.

King helped set this up as well. King was intent on being Pierre's agent when he left college. He rode the plane to Florida Prep, where Pierre would attend.

This was in the middle of Hurricane Katrina and the trip there and back was comprised by storms. We were fortunate to return home in one piece.

As I previously stated, prep school is an expensive venture. I did not have a job at the time and it had been years since I had given up the drug game so obviously I wasn't about to pay for it. I remember someone asking me, after we announced Pierre was headed off to prep school, how tough it would be to finance prep school. "You have to do what you have to do," I responded coyly. The truth: Calipari told me not to worry about it and that it would be taken care of. He was true to his word because I never spent a dime out of my pocket on tuition. I set it straight from the beginning with Cal, we can't afford prep school. I told him while sitting in his office with Pierre by my side. "We've got all of that," Cal said. "We've got that don't worry about that." He looked over at Pierre and instructed him to get out a sheet of paper and write out his goals. The first goal Pierre wrote was to come to Memphis and play. His second goal was to get to the NBA. "I've got you, I'm going to help you get there," Cal said of Pierre's NBA aspirations. "You need me and I need you and we're gonna get this done and I promise you, you're gonna be in the NBA. He told Pierre he could recall going to see Shawne Williams at an AAU game then being surprised by what he saw in Pierre, who put up thirty points with Williams guarding him. Cal told Pierre he remembered how he had it going that game, with a strong inside and outside presence. Pierre liked the sound of this. He also liked the sound of something else Calipari promised him that day, a car. And like most incoming students, Pierre wanted his high school jersey number. Those two promises never materialized. Pierre never received the car, and Willie Kemp would sport the number one on his jersey.

After this, Calipari and I never talked money or the "business" side of basketball. We would discuss Pierre and how he was progressing and things of that nature. Florida Prep was in deep water with the Florida High School Athletic Association for falsifying an official document and lost its membership with the organization. So we moved Pierre to another prep institution, the Patterson School in Lenior, North Carolina. While Pierre was in prep school, D.K. insisted that I not send money to Pierre. "We've got him taken care of," he would say. They did make sure he had money, still I sent him money anyway.

Pierre's weight issue was a concern of Calipari's and he would broach the topic without hitting it dead on. "Well Uncle Steve he can go play football if he wants to and sign a million dollar contract," he joked. Calipari would never throw harsh criticisms of Pierre while I was around, but a member of his staff would later tell me he road Pierre hard when I was out of the picture. The staff member could tell it was hurting Pierre's confidence to hear such direct and brutal criticism. I found it strange Calipari opened up his practices for the public to come in and watch the way he would go after players. His favorite target when Pierre arrived was forward Joey Dorsey, another Laurinburg Prep alum. During a scrimmage, Calipari got on one his players for passing the ball inside to Dorsey. Cal stopped the scrimmage and yelled, "We do not post Joey! Whatever you do, do not throw the ball inside to him." Meaning Dorsey would have to earn his shots from garbage efforts and put backs because Dorsey, 6-9 with a muscular chisel build, was not a good outside shooter. Dorsey was not his only target. He rode some of the other members of Pierre's class, like Kemp, Doneal Mack, and Tre'Von Willis. At times you could feel how uncomfortable it made visitors viewing the practice sessions.

Calipari had a practice that was uncommon in most coaching ranks; he always went after his players in front of the media. Most coaches downplay a players' negative attribute and uplift them with the positives ones. Yes, Calipari did praise players to the media but he would also criticize them just as quick. With Pierre he went after his weight. While in prep school Pierre played a lot of basketball, but he also ate a lot of fast food and started his freshman season at 310 pounds. His weight became an issue throughout his entire career at Memphis. Before his junior season, Cal pledged not to play him if he did not get down to a particular goal weight. Pierre worked his butt off each summer to slim down. During off season workouts, he was a beast; I don't say that because I'm his uncle, but because he would take it to guys like Dozier and Taggart. His outside shot was falling, his confidence was in full. Yet when the season came around, he was always looking over his shoulder wondering when he was going to be yanked. By his junior season, his psyche had gotten so bad that he grabbed an offensive rebound in a game and was wide open under the goal for a lay-up. Instead of going up with a shot, he passed it out to the perimeter. His confidence was totally shot.

Pierre called me near tears during his first year, right after the Tennessee game in Knoxville. He was devastated and embarrassed. The game was televised nationally on ESPN2 and Calipari played Pierre a grand total of six minutes, pulling him whenever he made a mistake. It was clear Pierre never had the chance to get comfortable in the game always looking over his shoulder wondering when he would be replaced. His state line looked like the baker's donut dozen, oooooo's all across. The Tigers were pounded that game, 76-58. Darius Washington, Sr, the father of Darius Jr., who played two years with the Tigers before deciding to go pro called me that night. He must have picked up on the energy via osmosis. "You better watch him," he said of Cal. "He's going to play mind games with Pierre. He's going to mess him over. He's going to try to turn him against you." I had gotten to know Darius, Sr. while the University of Memphis was pursuing Pierre. He was able to hip me on to some things early on. He asked me one day out of the blue, "How much money is he giving you?" I told him the truth. He told me he got all of his upfront. I had no idea where this money was coming from but let's be realistic, it had to be traced back to one person. And I don't know if he was getting this from a booster or was it coming from his own account, but if Pierre and I were getting a cut, I can only imagine what some of the other guys, the ones Cal actually played were receiving.

I thought the Tennessee game was just an isolated situation at first. I told him it would be okay, things would get better. "Keep working hard and do what you need to do. It will pay off. He's got to see it." But the situation turned into learned helplessness, meaning no matter what happened, Pierre knew the results, he would not see significant time on the floor. His stat line at the end of his freshman season read 0.2 points and 1 rebound a game. He played in 26 of their 40 games his sophomore season and averaged just 1.6 points and 2.2 rebounds. I felt for Pierre and Hashim "Big City" Bailey. Big City was also asked to lose weight, which he did, but did not see much of an increase in playing time. He eventually transferred to UMass to join D.K. I wanted Pierre to do the same. During his freshman year Pierre called me fifty times or more upset about how he felt he was being under-utilized at the school. Sometimes he would call or text me 3 or 4 times in a day. Sometimes I got messages.

"Man get me out of here."
"You need to come talk to these folks."
"What they're doing is bull."
"That man (Calipari) there…."

Of course Calipari's story was different. One day I walked into the Finch Center and Calipari motioned me over. I told him I needed to use the restroom first, but he was persistent. "I just want to tell you something right quick before somebody else does. All I said today is you can tell your uncle, your momma, your daddy whoever, I'm going to play you whenever I want to play you." Calipari said he was talking to the players in general about so-called outsiders and distractions. I ask Pierre about it and he told me after Calipari made the statement he told Dorsey he would share this bit of information with me because he felt Calipari was taking a jab at me. Dorsey told Calipari what Pierre said so I guess Calipari wanted to minimize the damage by telling me before Pierre could. Hmm. "Outsiders. Distractions." Those words from Calipari reminded me of something he told me about former player Darius Washington Jr. and his father. Before Pierre officially became a Tiger, Cal told me he was glad Darius and his troublemaking, overbearing father were no longer part of the program. He must have really felt threatened by family members concerned about the best interest of their loved ones.

Former Tigers' players Billy Richmond and Scooter McFadgon had both warned me about sending Pierre to Memphis. They didn't think it was a good idea but as I said before, going to Memphis was purely Pierre's.

I'll admit I just wanted Pierre out of there. People from the outside looking in, particularly sports radio host and callers, were saying Pierre should be happy because the Tigers were winning. You have to understand, yes young men want to win games, but more important they want to have fun. Having fun is feeling like you are part of the winning. Pierre did not feel that way. He took it in stride that his role would not be as monumental as he'd liked as a freshman, but as he continued to put in the time and work, he expected more and became frustrated when he didn't receive what he felt he earned. As a result, his morale was low; his confidence was replaced by confusion. Like anyone, Pierre did not like to be embarrassed, but with Calipari's in your face style during games, it was hard to avoid it. Calipari's rants at his players would often be heard on the television broadcasters' microphone, to the point where he would sometimes apologize to the viewing audience after the game. What he said during games was amplified to the third power during practices. Pussy, cocksucker, punks: those were all words used by Calipari to describe his very own players during his practices.

Pierre vented to me about Calipari on several occasions. "I can't do nothing. This man is always talking bad to me and cursing me out."

I was at practice one day when Pierre almost completely snapped. Calipari was criticizing him and Pierre shook his head as if he was just going to let the comment slide, then he came back at Cal. "Doesn't matter what I do, you're gonna pull me out of the game anyway. Let me make it easy for you and take myself out." Playing to the audience at the practice facility, Calipari replied, "Oh, so your uncle is here and now you want to bad mouth me." The truth is Pierre just wasn't good at hiding his frustrations. The few times the Tigers lost during his first three years, it was funny how the camera always managed to find him sitting on the bench with an intense look of frustration. When the Tigers lost the NCAA Championship game to Kansas in 2008, the cameras found him with his head in his hands hiding his face. Pierre did not touch the floor during that game. He could never hide the hurt. The money we were receiving didn't matter to me. It was not worth it. They could have it. I just wanted Pierre to be happy again, like he was in high school. I knew if I got him out of there the money would stop coming our way, but I didn't care anymore. I didn't want them to mess him over.

The worse part of it all is how my relationship with Pierre started to go south. During his sophomore season, Pierre again decided he had enough. I advised him, "Forget this money, and forget what they are giving us. Let's roll." He said he was ready and asked me to talk to some other college coaches to gauge their interest in him. "No problem," I told him. This time I cautioned him against being wishy-washy. "You can't keep doing me like this," I said to him, having me make these calls only for him to change his mind again. Coaches would ask me if I was sure he would transfer and to get back with them after he was released from his scholarship and held his news conference stating he was leaving.

Next thing I knew, I could not contact Pierre. He wouldn't answer his phone. My mom even called him asking him why he wouldn't pick up the phone. "What has your uncle ever done to you that would cause you to treat him like that?" she asked. He would at least answer her phone calls. I'm sure he did not want to hear from me because I would get on him. Pierre wouldn't even make eye contact with me when I came by the team's practices. I had no idea what was going on. Kemp was even in my corner. He remembered all I had done for his AAU squad, confronting the Adidas people to make sure the team had their gear and hotel money. In addition I was helpful in getting DK in good with Kemp. I told Kemp Calipari's coaching staff was on the take. I arranged for the two to talk. I'm not sure what happened after that. He tried talking some sense into Pierre. Still we became more distant. I surmised word had reached Calipari of my plans of getting Pierre out of Memphis and maybe he continued his theme of keeping out the "distractions." I had no choice but to give Pierre his space. I quit calling for a period of time and just assumed and hoped, he would come around. But one thing that did not change from his freshman to sophomore season was me showing up at his home games and supporting him. I would also give him money, $300 to $400 at a time. "They" had stopped funneling money Pierre's way, although "they" continued to share the wealth me as we agreed upon.

Before his senior year our relationship improved. Right after the Tigers lost to Missouri in the Sweet Sixteen during his junior season he called telling me he would give my number to a workout specialist in Boston name Bobby Martin. He invited me to head out East with Pierre, but I had too much going on at my church to even entertain it. Martin told me he thought Pierre had NBA potential and was looking forward to working with him. But once Calipari decided to leave for Lexington, Pierre decided to stay in Memphis during the summer and workout on his own. I got on him. "Why," I asked, "would you give me the man's number if you were not going to take my advice and go up there?" To his credit he worked hard and dropped off so much weight he looked like the Pierre of Ridgeway.

When Calipari left, so did some of the Tigers' recruits, leaving new coach Josh Pastner with only a handful of scholarship players. One would have to be crazy to think Memphis would be as successful as they were during the later years of Calipari under the current circumstances. If there was a silver lining in the shakeup, it was that guys like Niles, Mack, and Kemp would get a chance to finally prove they were good players.

Pierre worked so hard during the off season. We knew it would be a special one. He began the season in the starting lineup. As the year progressed it was much of the same under Pastner. Two coaches, same issue. Of course people began to think maybe it was Pierre. But the damage had already been done. When Pastner started giving him the Calipari treatment, he was not sure how to handle it. He just assumed the worse. Early on in his senior season

Pierre told Josh he was leaving the team. Josh called me constantly telling me how they needed Pierre. I told Josh he was doing Pierre just like Calipari and not letting him play through his mistakes. Both Josh and I were genuine when we told Pierre he needed to play his senior year; so Pierre decided to commit himself to the team for another season. But with eight games remaining in the regular season, Pierre and Pastner decided it was the best thing for both parties to go their separate ways.

I was hurt and disappointed at the same time. I knew how this would cripple his already fragile perception with the public, but he also let his teammates down. People may think I'm bitter by Pierre's journey at the University of Memphis and that is not true. Now I'm not at all pleased with his career at Memphis, but at the same time I'm mature enough to accept accountability and responsibility. Pierre could have done some things to improve his own situation. Plan and simple Pierre quit and that's the last thing he needed to do. He did not stick around to face the media and talk about his decision. It's a shame what he endured at that school with all the hard work he put in. I'm certain if he could get a redo he would decide to stick it out, but life doesn't always grant you a makeover.

People need to know how young men in this whole college system are used and then tossed to the side. They all have dreams of playing professionally some day and of course everyone is not going to make it even if their coaches tell them otherwise. Regardless if they play by the rules or not, the student athlete is usually the one who suffers long term, the one left out in the cold. But what happens to the corrupt coach? There are so many basketball players who have played for Calipari that have a similar story. But a cycle exists.

See, no one will ever come forward because by doing so they are incriminating themselves in the process. I know of other stories within that program under Calipari as does several others. But someone has to tell the truth and who knows, with me starting the relay, maybe there will be others willing to accept the baton and help put an end to the madness. I would be willing to tell my story while hooked up to a lie-detector device, you think Calipari and members of his staff would be willing to do the same?

One thing that would help end the corrupt practices is if these young men, pushing their bodies to the limit, bringing in all of this money to universities, would be allowed to be paid above the table. When you are performing for people at that level, you should be getting paid. Everyone gets filthy rich off the dedication and hard work of these athletes except the athletes themselves. Something about that just seems wrong.

Looking Back, Moving Forward

For my thoughts are not your thoughts, neither are your ways my ways, saith the LORD. Isaiah 55:8

It's good to look back over your life and thank God for all the good days and for what you may consider as bad days. While incarcerated, I had an opportunity to repent. That one act changed my life forever. It took incarceration, but I developed a relationship with God. In the past, I guided myself. I learned to put God first and foremost in my life and lean and depend on Him. I found that there are no regrets in God only hope, love, and a bright future.

As I was driving East on Interstate 70 traveling from the Raleigh Memphis area to Mason, the place where some of my most memorable and forgettable moments occurred, I could not help but to reflect on how much things in this small town remained the same but at the same time how so much had changed.

Police still hide out looking to find someone speeding through. What were once miles and miles of rural land had been changed to grocery stores, gas stations, and mini-marts. Most people taking the drive would look at it as a chore, but for me back in my days of infamy, it was always a time to relax, the calm before the storm. I can recall leading a fleet of vehicles to Mason for a night or weekend of utter chaos.

I remember approaching the town of Gallaway and knowing that only Braden City separated me from Mason. Leaders in the town of Mason brag of it being the birthplace of Isaac Hayes as it is displayed on the very first sign within city limits as you approach it from I-70.

This time when I finally enter Mason I noticed for the first time the huge water tower landmark that reads "established 1855." Funny I never paid attention to that while I was hustling and bustling there in the '80s and '90s. Back then the first thing I would notice as soon as I turned on Main Street from Highway 70 was the car wash center packed with cars leading all the way up the strip of clubs lining out to the length of a football field. We all knew it was on at that point.

Once you found a parking space about twenty-minutes later, it was always entertaining to keep track of all the automobile tags registered from out of state. Vehicles from Michigan, Illinois, Mississippi, Arkansas, Texas, and Missouri on various weekends had all descended on Mason to party with us. The clubs were elevated above the main parking lot.

The very first club in viewing distance as we turned on Front street from Main was the Real Deal, then the Brown Hut, followed by House Party and my mom's old club, the Red Hut,, then the Blue Lantern, which my mom co-owned and managed before the Red Hut. The Pool Hall was west of Blue Lantern and followed by three other clubs before you get to the Green Hut and finally the Black Hut. Black Hut was a café for the older crowd, people in their 50s and beyond. The clubs were like a Cliff Notes' version of Bourbon Street.

There was a small cotton factory next to the strip and several of the employees would leave work at night and walk right on over. They had the advantage of having a great parking space of course. Just south of the clubs ran a railroad track and being on the wrong side of the track when a train was coming through was being on the side opposite the clubs.

Today all that's left of those clubs are large slabs of concrete without a hint of anything resembling revitalization of the area. I've always assumed the reason the club scene in Mason became extinct was the increased competition from neighboring towns opening bars and places to dance. Plus club owners like my mom decided to move on from all of the drama. Some of today's residents of Mason believe it has a great deal to do with the town's current mayor. Accordingly he wanted to change the town's image and get rid of all of the clubs.

For the most part, the people of Mason were great. Some would do anything for you. Even to this day. As I was passing through and getting a renewed feel for the place that was once my second home, I passed by Alexander AME Church, the place I had visited several times before in the past and stopped my car to get a refresher look. As I was glancing at the church I noticed a man and a woman at the house next door on the front lawn talking. I'm thinking to myself, that guy looks familiar. In fact he looked like a guy who always looked out for the youngsters in Mason, Butch. So I drove closer and I noticed the two cut off their conversation and started looking in my direction. The smiles on their faces soon turned into a look of concern. I had to get out and check. I pulled up in the driveway, walked up to the gentleman who didn't take his eyes off me the entire time. I could tell he sensed trouble. I asked him if his name was Butch. He didn't say a word. The woman in the yard chimed in, "Butch died." For a brief moment I was frozen by the statement. Then I looked over at the gentleman again then proclaimed, "No way, that's Butch," I said looking in the direction of the man and I started laughing. "You don't remember me?" I asked him. "It's Little Steve." Then I dropped my mom's name on him. The smile soon came back. The woman was a friend and longtime Mason resident name Ray. Like Butch, she sensed trouble and with her protective instincts said he had passed away. They did not recognize me immediately because I no longer had gold teeth in my mouth, nor did I have the curl chemicals that had been my trademark back when. We all had a good laugh about it once I identified myself. See, the good people of Mason still have each other's back.

Butch is now in his late 50s or early 60s. He was wearing a camouflage jacket, an old pair of jeans and his knuckles had signs of wear. He held on to a bottle container wrapped in a brown paper grocery store bag. He and Ray smiled often, laughed often, particularly when we talked about the "good ole" days. Butch's memory is like that of an elephant, he was recalling events and times as if he was pulling them from the air. While we were all reminiscing, Ray's husband Ricky Fletcher drove up.

Ricky was the only white police officer I knew well during my notorious days in Mason. As you can imagine, I had my differences with law enforcers at that time, but Ricky was always fair to me and he was particularly fond of my mom. As anyone would expect after more than a decade, Ricky is a bit thicker. He still owns that Deep South accent, and his face is now hardened and skin cracked perhaps

Flagrant Fouls

by the constant use of nicotine. He laughs about my previous run-ins with the law now and says he knew we were gambling in those clubs years ago, but he preferred for us to be in one location not causing any real trouble then spreading about town causing unknown mayhem.

We had a system at my mom's club for when Ricky or any other police officer would drop in. We had this jerry-rigged light system that I would pull in the front of the club that would shine in the back where all the gambling was taking place, alerting the customers of the presence of cops. One day Ricky caught me in the act, "I know what you're doing Steve," he told me. He and I both joke about it now. I believe if Ricky were not a police officer and did not have to patrol the area, he would have been a regular at those clubs to just enjoy himself. The day I returned to Mason he was going on and on about all the great musical acts who passed through the town performing at those establishments. "I remember when Rufus Thomas performed here," he bragged, "Clarence Carter," he continued. Then he started rattling off some of the local rap-artist that paraded in....like Project Pat whom he described as "polite as he can be," or Skinny Pimp, whom he and I both remember trying to get away with door money at club House Party shortly after performing at my mom's club one night. Ricky and some of the other officers were after him like a greyhound on a track rabbit. Fortunately they caught him and recovered the money.

I asked Ray about a guy who use to stay in trouble named Carl. She told me he's gotten his life back after changing his habits and pushing away the bottle. Like my own, his life is proof there's hope for everybody.

Ray confesses she's a big fan of John Calipari and is not surprised he was so successful with the University of Kentucky during his first season in Lexington. Butch doesn't share her sentiments. He still harbors ill feelings with all that went down after Calipari left "Memphis State." Everybody embraces the team, but some have yet to accept "University of Memphis" as the name. But I'm willing to bet the majority share the opinion of Butch as it relates to Calipari.

It was a very disappointing finish to the NCAA Tournament for Calipari and his Wildcats. They were bumped out in their Elite Eight round against West Virginia. Afterward, basketball critics took Calipari to task about his coaching again. He was dogged for not being able to adjust to the Mountaineers plan. Oddly both he and West Virginia's coach Bobby Huggins are two of the primary names that pop up when people talk about the best coach to never win it all, further adding to Calipari's legacy of being a great recruiter but less than stellar x and o instructor.

I imagine it will be hard for him to do what he did in his first year at Kentucky and win 30-plus games, win the SEC regular season title, win the SEC Tournament, and make a solid run in the tournament because in early April of 2010, five of his players declared for the NBA Draft. One player, freshman John Wall, was expected to be the number one overall pick. DeMarcus Cousins, another freshman is projected to go in the top 5 but as high as second. Three of the players will be lottery picks but all are said to be first round selections. If they hold true to their plans, Kentucky will have some major rebuilding to do. It is not easy to replace that kind of talent; still Calipari met with each player and encouraged them to test the NBA waters. If this sounds familiar it's because it's similar to the scenario back in 2008 when after falling one game short on their NCAA Championship bid, Derek Rose decided to leave after his freshman season, Chris Douglas-Roberts departed as a junior and Antonio Anderson and Robert Dozier, who also completed their third year, submitted their names for draft consideration. Like Anderson and Dozier would change their tune and return to school.

Before leaving Mason I had to stop by the place that helped put the town on the map to begin with, Gus' Fried Chicken. The place is renowned across the nation. There are only about seven locations, all located in the Mid-South. And to think it all started in Mason. I don't know what they do to those birds but the finished product is amazing. I was the first patron there that day, arriving just moments before they opened at 10 a.m. and beating the lunch rush.

While I waited for my food, Carl, of all people showed up. Ray and I had just spoken about him and presto he appears at Gus'. Just like Butch, he didn't know who I was until I told him I removed the grill from my mouth. Ray was right about Carl; he had all his senses about him. He was in good spirits and moving in the right direction. Seeing Carl in his right state of mind was the highlight of my return to Mason.

Heading back to Memphis I couldn't help but to think of my nephew, Pierre. We had gone through some tough times while he was playing at Memphis. Our relationship began to strengthen again when he left the team. On Easter Sunday he showed up at church. I believe he began to understand that God, followed by family, is more important than anything else in this world. Once again we can talk basketball and more important we can talk about life. Hopefully he understands through all the mistakes I have made in life, taking him in was not one of them. I love that man-child like he cannot fully understand at this point in his life.

Pierre has not given up on his dream of playing in the NBA. He knows it will not be easy. Things will get tougher for him now because basketball has tipped the scales of being more business than pleasure. He will look to basketball to provide him with a living. He's hired an agent and will take the unconventional approach to getting to the league and attempt to find a job playing basketball overseas first. If Pierre keeps his priorities in line, he should be able to actualize his dreams. God first. He made a huge stride to do that Saturday, May 8th 2010 when he walked across the stage at the same place he played his home games as a Tiger, FedEx Forum. He received his Interdisciplinary Studies Degree and will always have something to fall back on.

My dream remains to get my congregation into a building of our own. We're not asking for anything big and fancy because church is not about where you worship, but who you worship with. It's about spreading and sharing the word with as many people as possible. Last decades recession spilled over into this one. It forced many churches to shut their physical doors, but it didn't stop the Lord's people from doing ministry work. Some houses of the Lord fortunate enough to maintain their place of worship open their place during non-hours of operation to churches without a physical place to gather. My church benefited from such generosity. But that's just an example of the Lord at work for you. Where there's a will there's a way, the Lord's Will. When we get a building of our own we will pass along the blessing and assist someone else.

Regrets? Not many because life is all about experiences. If I have any regrets it's that I didn't use my time wisely when I was out on the streets selling drugs. I wasn't looking at getting something solid and concrete down the road for myself. I should have been getting an education. Still I know now my life is drawing people to me based on my experience. People know they can come to me as their pastor because I've been through the struggles and understand how to overcome and rely on God. Some preachers are behind the pulpit for the popularity, the prestige, the power, and the money. They are in it for the wrong reason. The bible says many are called but few are chosen. My experiences have taught me a lot about myself and a lot about life. Prison was God sitting me down so he could talk to me and explain his plan. Had I not ended up behind bars, I could have been dead.

As I look back on the wrong I've done, the mistakes I've made, I'm fortunate by only the grace of God to have escaped the trials and tribulations of my past life. Unlike a lot of young adults today, who believe they are victims of the system, I understand I have myself to blame for it. Still I know I went through it all for a reason. I've come out of it a soldier, stronger than ever before. I'm now in a position to help so many others understand life and avoid the hazards I met dead on. Understand I did not find peace of mind until I gave myself to the Lord 100-percent.

Amen.

About the Author

Stephen A. Saine is a native of the bluff city Memphis, Tennessee, where he still resides. Currently the pastor of Higher Heights Christian Church, Saine's rise from street hustler to Man of God is chronicled in his first book offering, *Flagrant Fouls*. Saine escaped narrow calls to answer his calling as preacher and hopes to be a source of inspiration to those who have taken the wrong road in life. He wants them to know they can also get on the right path.

Saine is a husband, a father, a son, a brother, friend, but more importantly a humble servant of Christ.

www.ingramcontent.com/pod-product-compliance
Lightning Source LLC
LaVergne TN
LVHW041544070426
835507LV00011B/924